Yeats
the
Playwright

A Commentary on
Character and Design
in the Major Plays

by

PETER URE

Routledge & Kegan Paul
London

First published 1963
by Routledge and Kegan Paul Ltd
Broadway House, 68-74 Carter Lane
London, E.C.4
Reprinted 1969
Reprinted by photolithography in Great Britain
by Bookprint Limited, Crawley, Sussex
SBN 7100 2351 0(c)
SBN 7100 6550 7(p)

Contents

Preface

SINCE my first book on Yeats was published sixteen years ago I have learnt much from many distinguished students of Yeats's poetry; but to Birgit Bjersby (*The Interpretation of the Cuchulain Legend in the Works of W. B. Yeats*), Giorgio Melchiori (articles later incorporated in his *The Whole Mystery of Art*), Thomas Parkinson (*W. B. Yeats: Self-Critic*), and F. A. C. Wilson (*W. B. Yeats and Tradition*), all of whom have written at length on the plays, I am more particularly indebted in the writing of this book. I regret that Mr. Wilson's second book, *Yeats's Iconography* appeared after the greater part of my work was done, as did an excellent brief account, with superb illustrations, by D. J. Gordon and Ian Fletcher, in *W. B. Yeats: Images of a Poet*. Some portions of this book (Chapter I in part, Chapter III, Chapter VI, and a section of Chapter VII) have appeared previously in periodicals and I am grateful to the editors and publishers of *The Modern Language Review*, *English Studies*, *The Review of English Studies*, and *The Huntington Library Quarterly* for permission to revise and reprint them. Thanks are due to the following for permission to reprint copyright material: Mrs. W. B. Yeats and Messrs. Macmillan and Co. for passages from the works of W. B. Yeats; Mrs. Yeats and Rupert Hart-Davis for passages from *The Letters of W. B. Yeats*, edited by Allan Wade; Messrs. Faber and Faber for a passage from *The Translations of Ezra Pound*.

P. U.

Introduction

YEATS's plays have not, generally speaking, been much regarded by his modern critics. They have tended to judge the earlier ones (1889-1906) as flaccid and sentimental, and the later ones (1915-38) as barbarous, remote, theatrically impractical, or merely puzzling. This commentary attempts to consider their strengths and weaknesses in plot, characterization, and the handling of morals and ideas. The unit of discussion throughout the book is the individual play. This method has been chosen because it seemed the best way of making the book a supplement to the reading of the plays themselves. No one reads through the *Collected Plays* from start to finish except at the risk of bewilderment and mental indigestion. But a reader may look at a play here and there in the volume, or study a group of like-minded plays, and he may then find it useful to test his impressions by a critical account of what he has read. What is offered here, therefore, is a critical handbook or companion to some features of the plays rather than an attempt to judge and arrange them all in the light of a dominant theory.

The arrangement adopted recognizes that the plays tend to be read in groups, although these will not necessarily be the same for every reader, or constituted on the same principles. The order of discussion is not, except in the first and shorter Part, a chronological one, but I have supplied in an Appendix a brief guide to the order in which the plays were written, performed, and printed. In the second Part the plays are grouped according to theme and subject-matter: Cuchulain, life-in-death, Christianity, the Unicorn and the 'beast' (the last collocation I borrow from Professor G. Melchiori). This method seems to avoid the risk of there being too much repetition in what it is necessary to say about Yeats's philosophical mythology. It is also, of course, a risk to put together into the same chapter plays which differ from one another in form so clearly as do, for example, *Purgatory* and *The Words upon the Window-pane*; but it sometimes makes it possible to stress the formal experimentation and variety which Yeats went in for when he was writing for the theatre, and, it is hoped, to bring out important differences in construction and characterization.

I have also felt free, as a commentator, rather than a writer with any very confident prepossessions about what modern poetic drama ought to be, to consider these groups of plays with the aid of techniques and criteria which are not necessarily compatible with one another. These have been applied where they were most useful and then abandoned even when to continue to apply them would have seemed more thorough and consistent. Thus, in the first two chapters, on *The Countess Cathleen* and *The King's Threshold*, there is a great deal about the variant texts of these two heavily revised plays. Study of the revisions could have been continued on much the same scale for a number of other plays, because Yeats was a constant reviser of his plays as of his poems, but the character of his work in this kind is such that the result would have been more of a book about Yeats as a reviser than a companion to the reading of his plays. But I wanted to discuss other matters as well in the chapters that follow: the relation between dramatic theory and dramatic practice in Chapter III, Yeats as an ironist in Chapter IV, the relation (and the difference) between the philosophical mythologist and the playwright in Chapter V, between remoteness and realism in Chapter VI, between theme and image in Chapter VII. All these—and many others suggest themselves—are matters which could be used to establish a thesis which might hold good for all of the plays. Perhaps one or other of them is the ingenious tool which could force Yeats to divulge his secret. But none of them is pursued here to more than a provisional conclusion because it seems more important at the present stage of Yeats's reputation as a playwright to subordinate them to an attempt to describe one by one the organization of the plays. The naïvete and eclecticism of this manner of proceeding, together with its inevitable mass of unexamined and unconscious critical assumptions, may justly displease those who feel that the time has come for Yeats to be firmly placed in the history of the development of poetic drama. But this book is written in the conviction that Yeats's plays—even those earlier ones which are now dismissed as pseudo-Elizabethan or post-Maeterlinckian, and certainly those later ones of which the last were written only a couple of decades ago—need to be lived with a little longer as individual works of art, and more intensively than they have been, before they are fitted into any consistent scheme.

It is for similar reasons that I have not written about the poetry of the plays as such. A great deal of material lies ready to hand for such an exercise, not least those transpositions from prose into verse represented by alternative versions of *The Hour-Glass, The Golden Helmet, The King of the Great Clock Tower*, and other plays or portions of plays. But sooner or later any enquiry runs foul of current arguments about the principles, needs, and desirability of poetic drama on the modern stage. No one can deny the probable relevance of Yeats's precepts and practice to these arguments; but both are of such a kind that they will be found more often to conflict than to accord with the formulae at present dominant, nearly all of which have been contrived by Mr. Eliot, the other great poet of the century who has written poetry for the English-speaking stage. Yeats, for example, was willing to mingle verse and prose in the same play, and this directly contravenes one of Eliot's laws; he often wrote Shakespearian or Jacobean blank verse (when it is not more like Dryden's), and whether this was a fatal error or a just and natural recognition of its usefulness can hardly be discussed until the rigour which is appeased only by the employment of non-Shakespearian rhythms can be relaxed. Disagreements of this kind are so far-reaching that, although separation must, in the end, appear artificial, they are best handled independently of the attempt to describe construction, theme, and character.

The term 'major plays', although evaluative, is not intended to be taken very seriously as such, but chiefly as an indication that not all the plays are discussed here. I have left out *The Island of Statues* (1885) and *Mosada* (1886), the juvenile lyrical dramas which Yeats did not reprint in the definitive edition of his poetry. Of the other plays written before 1906, I have omitted *The Land of Heart's Desire, Cathleen ni Houlihan, The Hour-Glass, The Pot of*

3

Broth, and *The Shadowy Waters*. The first and the last of these seem too closely connected with the poetry of that time to be usefully discussed independently of it, and *The Shadowy Waters* has also had the advantage of a very full treatment in Professor Parkinson's *W. B. Yeats Self-Critic* (1951); the others are best thought of in relation to the full reassessment of the work of Lady Gregory that one hopes will some day be written. I have discussed at greater or less length all the plays written or finished after 1915, except *The Cat and the Moon* and the translations from Sophocles.

It is, unfortunately, the reader rather than the theatregoer who has to assume the burden of deciding whether or not they are 'major' in a grander sense. It is difficult to make bold claims for them as plays for the theatre, because the modern theatre has simply decided that they cannot be fitted in. This judgement would be more worthy of respect if it did not extend to the work of such masters of the stage and audience as Jonson, Middleton, and (on this side of the Atlantic) Shaw. It is more understandable in the case of Yeats, who created his own instrument and traditions, which were dissipated when their constituent persons went their ways.

> But actors lacking music
> Do most excite my spleen,
> They say it is more human
> To shuffle, grunt and groan,
> Not knowing what unearthly stuff
> Rounds a mighty scene,
> > *Said the man in the golden breastplate*
> > *Under the old stone Cross.*

But there is still the obligation, entailed upon those who wish to understand his art, to try to measure his plays by those criteria, infinitely slippery though they are, which are appropriate to works written for performance by actors before an audience. It is at least an important fact about this great lyric poet that he should have continued to labour so long at 'plays That have to be set up in fifty ways', and that he should have felt that he *needed* a theatre:

I believe myself to be a dramatist; I desire to show events and not merely tell of them; and two of my best friends were won for me

4

Introduction

---

by my plays, and I seem to myself most alive at the moment when a room full of people share the one lofty emotion.

It is possible that the dramatist in Yeats was merely the stalking-horse of the symbolist poet and the philosophical mythologist. But the evidence, though it is far from clear, is also far from being all in favour of that opinion, and it is hoped that this book gives some reasons why.

If this book can serve at all as a supplement, it is intended for *The Collected Plays of W. B. Yeats*, first issued in 1934 (second enlarged edition 1952), the only collection still kept in print. For various reasons, such as the need to investigate variant texts, and Yeats's Introductions and Notes (all omitted from *Collected Plays*), my work has normally been with the earlier editions, of which the most important are *Four Plays for Dancers* (1921), *Plays . . . for an Irish Theatre* (1922), *Plays and Controversies* (1923), and *Wheels and Butterflies* (1934), all now out of print. The student will presumably need to consult these on occasions when the general reader does not. My quotations are normally from the texts in the volumes named and in others earlier still. Although, when discussing a particular play in the section or chapter devoted to it, I have always indicated which text (or texts) of it I am using, I have not usually supplied a page-reference for each successive quotation from the play under discussion. This has been done in order to avoid an excessive accumulation of such references and in the belief that, because the plays are so short, it is not difficult for readers wishing to look up the passage in its context to find it in *Collected Plays* or in one of the other volumes. References for all quotations and allusions not of this particular kind are of course supplied.

5

PART ONE:
APPLIED ARTS

I disliked the isolation of the work of art. I wished
through the drama, through a commingling of verse
and dance, through singing that was also speech,
through what I called the applied arts of literature,
to plunge it back into social life.

—*Pages from a Diary*
Written in Nineteen Hundred and Thirty

Chapter One

A Counter-Truth

I

'YEATS was there, listening reverentially to the sound of his own verses', wrote George Moore in *Ave*, and went on to give an account of his own sensations during the famous first week of *The Countess Cathleen* in May, 1899. Writing ten years after the event, he was able to charge them with that delightful note of ironic bewilderment which became him so well and made the fortune of his masterpiece. Earlier, he had written more brutally about the defects of the performance:

The Countess Cathleen met with every disadvantage. Here is a list which must not, however, be considered exhaustive. First, the author's theory that verse should be chanted and not spoken; second, the low platform insufficiently separated from the audience; third, a set of actors and actresses unaccustomed to speak verse; fourth, harsh, ridiculous scenery; fifth, absurd costumes. . . . Many times I prayed during the last act that the curtain might come down at once.[1]

Although Moore was unimpressed by the group of professional players which Florence Farr had brought from London, including the young May Whitty in the part of the Countess, he claimed that the intense beauty of the play was not completely obscured by its representation. In the gloomy, improvised Dublin concert room it awakened in him 'just such a sense of beauty as I have experienced in dim museums, looking at some worn and broken bas-relief'.

The police were present—twenty men and a sergeant, according to Yeats[2]—to discourage those who, stimulated by the pamphlet *Souls for Gold! Pseudo-Celtic Drama in Dublin*, were determined to suppress heresy:

The accusation made was that it was a libel on the people of Ireland to say they could under any circumstances consent to sell their souls and that it was a libel on the demons that they counted the soul of a countess more worth than those of the poor.[3]

There were other signs that the occasion was historic. The Dublin *Daily Express*, under the editorship of T. P. Gill, had during that same month of May reprinted as a booklet the contributions which John Eglinton, Yeats, and A. E. had made to its columns the previous autumn about whether or not the ancient Irish legends constituted proper material for a modern Irish poet. A. E. had closed the discussion with his argument that to use the heroic legends was to fight on behalf of Irish nationality against the cosmopolitan spirit which was rapidly obliterating all distinctions. Such an obliterator, according to A. E., was Professor Dowden. Yeats, with greater circumspection, had named Goethe, Wordsworth, and Browning as poets of utilitarianism and rhetoric, through whom poetry had given up 'the right to consider all things in the world as a dictionary of types and symbols'. 'The other path'—so ran A. E.'s appeal—the path of nationality and myth and dream,

winds spirally upwards to a mountain-top of our own, which may be in the future the Meru to which many worshippers will turn.[4]

'This was a stirring row', Yeats commented later, '. . . and we were all very angry'.[5] Nationality, *The Countess Cathleen*, and the Irish themes were at the same time making an appeal of some historic importance to two other members of the audience in the Antient Concert Rooms: the brothers William and Frank Fay were more magnanimous than George Moore:

We liked it very much and thought the company gave an excellent performance, one thing being very noticeable—the admirable delivery

10

of Mr. Yeats's verse, which was not so speakable then as in his later plays for he had had little experience of writing for the stage. . . . It was this performance of *The Countess Cathleen* that first suggested the idea of the company that eventually became known as the Irish Players. When Frank and I left the hall we were enthusiastic about what we had just seen. We had enough personal experience to be able to allow for the loss the play suffered through having its production on a 'fit-up' stage and in a hall that was not intended for dramatic entertainment. Yet even so there seemed to be something missing. What was it? Then it suddenly flashed upon me that what was wrong with the performance was that, though the artists were most efficient, they were not Irish. To get the full value of the play one must have native actors. . . . Frank quite agreed with me, but he very pertinently asked, 'Where in Ireland could you get any company of actors that could compare with those we have just seen?' [6]

It was because the Fays, Yeats, and Lady Gregory contrived to answer this question between them that Yeats got, for a lifetime at least, access to a living theatre.

All that glory and excitement have faded now, and *The Countess Cathleen*, with its careful piety and mannered exaltation, has faded too. 'It was not, nor is it now, more than a piece of tapestry,' Yeats remarked.[7] As it lies folded in the mouth of the standard edition of the Collected Plays, dated 1892 with seriously misleading pedantry, it is a dragon without much fire left in its belly. But an examination of its genesis and history still has something to reveal about Yeats as a dramatic craftsman. An intelligible map of the first of his two phases of dramatic work, that which extends from *The Countess Cathleen* to *Deirdre*, cannot be drawn without such aid as it supplies. In the help it gives towards delineating the phase, which comprises only four other major plays (*The Shadowy Waters*, *On Baile's Strand*, *The King's Threshold*, *Deidre*), it shows how Yeats came to recognize, despite a good deal of resistance, some of the limits and bounds of his craft.

II

The reverence and intentness which Moore observed in Yeats as he listened to Florence Farr and her company arose from Yeats's determination to discover what could and could not be done in the theatre. He wrote towards the end of his first period as playwright:

Every one who has to interest his audience through the voice discovers that his success depends upon the clear, simple and varied structure of his thought. I have written a good many plays in verse and prose, and almost all those plays I have rewritten after performance, sometimes again and again, and every re-writing that has succeeded upon the stage has been an addition to the masculine element, an increase of strength in the bony structure.[8]

Describing Yeats's evolution as a playwright would be a simpler business than it is if this and similar observations could be taken as a safe guide through the labyrinth of the different versions of *The Countess Cathleen*. All that it would then be necessary to do would be to look for and acclaim the gradual emergence of structural order out of the monotony and effeminacy and 'strained lyricism' for which Yeats in the same passage censured William Morris, contrasting *The Earthly Paradise* with *The Canterbury Tales* and blaming Morris for being 'too continuously lyrical in his understanding of emotion and life'. And much later, Yeats described the 1889 version of *The Countess Cathleen* as 'ill-constructed, the dialogue turning aside at the lure of word or metaphor, very different, I hope, from the play as it is to-day after many alterations, every alteration tested by performance'.[9]

The history of *The Countess Cathleen*, so far as it can be examined by means of the printed texts, does not entirely confirm this version of events. There were in the revisions of the play more indirection and resistance and regression than will admit of any very clear progress from lyrical effeminacy to masculine strength. Sometimes, indeed, the expected process seems to go into reverse; a structure originally simple and clear might become blurred with afterthoughts or strained out of shape by fresh insights. It is a story of loss as well as gain. The gain is hardly to be measured by any version, even the final version (if finality was ever reached) of *The Countess Cathleen* itself, but by what Yeats achieved when he tackled fresh themes and abandoned for the time the Countess's singularly obdurate story.

The version which aroused such passions in the Antient Concert Rooms was the third of five major revisions. The record of revision,* extending over nearly thirty years, is lengthier than that of *The Shadowy Waters* or of any other play by Yeats. Only an edition which printed all the *varia* could justly show the full extent of the minor alterations, which are by no means confined to the four occasions, in 1895, 1901, 1912, and 1919, when the play underwent major revision. But I shall confine this discussion mostly to the first version and to the first text of each of its four successors. The table on pages 14–15 is a convenient, if graceless, way of providing a basis for considering how much, and how little, the alterations affected the story, shape, and construction of the play.

Its genesis was laborious, from March, 1889, until October, 1891. Various references to it in the letters show that it was from the first conceived as a stage-play, never as a purely lyrical drama. There were two other matters that influenced its design in 1889–92. The first of these was the idea of it as a counter or contrast to the recently published *Wanderings of Oisin* (1889). In 1892 Yeats wrote of the play as:

an attempt to mingle personal thought and feeling with the beliefs and customs of Christian Ireland; whereas the longest poem in my earlier book endeavoured to set forth the impress left on my imagination by the Pre-Christian cycle of legends. The Christian cycle being mainly concerned with contending moods and moral motives needed,

---

* Yeats planned out and began to write *The Countess Cathleen* in February/March, 1889 (*Letters*, pp. 108, 114), and it was first printed in *The Countess Kathleen and Various Legends and Lyrics* (1892). In March, 1894, *The Land of Heart's Desire* was presented in London as a curtain-raiser for *Arms and the Man*. It was the first play by Yeats to be produced on any stage. In the light of this experience Yeats revised and expanded the earlier play and printed this version in *Poems*,1895. The play was again revised for the Dublin production in 1899; this version, the third, was printed for the first time in *Poems*, 1901. (A copy of *Poems*, 1899, in the Huntington Library preserves the autograph revisions made for the performance, and the Huntington also has the typescript of the enlarged third Act: see Parkinson, p. 188.) This version appeared in *Poems*, 1904, in *The Poetical Works of William B. Yeats* (New York, 1907), in *Poems*, 1908, and, for the last time, in volume III of the Stratford-on-Avon *Collected Works* (1908). The fourth version—which is sometimes erroneously described as the final version (for example, by Henn, p. 30)—was first printed in 1912 as Volume I of 'Dublin Plays 'and in *Poems*, 1912. After this the play was revised again: the texts in *Poems* 1919, and *Plays and Controversies* (1923) represent this fifth version.

13

REVISION OF THE COUNTESS CATHLEEN

*A: This indicates scenes in which Aleel (Kevin in 1892) appears

1892 Countess Kathleen and Various Legends and Lyrics	1895 Poems, 1895 & 1899	1901 Poems, 1901, 1904, 1908, Poetical Works (New York), 1907, Collected Works (Stratford-on-Avon), 1908	1912 'Dublin Plays' edition and Poems, 1912	1919 Poems, 1919 Plays & Controversies, 1923 Collected Plays, 1934, &c.
SCENE I — The inn of Shemus Rua called 'The Lady's Head'; the starving family (Shemus, Mary and their son Teig); the entry of the two Demon-Merchants and their offer to buy souls.	ACT I *A — *Adds* entry of the Countess with Aleel; her charity; Aleel's song ('Impetuous heart, be still').	ACT I *A	SCENE I *A — *Completely re-written, but with episodes as in 1895.*	SCENE I *A — *New song for Aleel ('Were I but crazy for love sake') replaces 'Impetuous heart, be still'.*
SCENE II — The Castle Hall; the Countess and Oona; servants bring news of theft and disorder; two peasants bring news of the traffic in souls; the Countess instructs her steward to sell her lands and distribute her money to all suppliants.	ACT II [Part i]	ACT II — *Adds* (at beginning of the Act) the love-scene for the Countess and Aleel.	SCENE II *A — *Completely re-written, using episodes of 1892 in shorter form. Adds new scene for Aleel, Countess of Oona in place of passages for Countess and Oona only in 1892.*	SCENE II *A
SCENE III — The Castle Hall; the Demon-Merchants discuss their progress so far; they rob the	ACT II [Part ii]	ACT III *A	SCENE III *A — *Robbery-scene re-written in shortened form.*	SCENE III *A — *Robbery scene cut to a few words and actions; all supernatural aides eliminated.*

treasure-house and summon spirits and lost souls to aid them in carrying away the bags of treasure; the Countess enters and talks with them about the state of the land; but their identity is not recognized until the theft is discovered after they have left; the Countess gives her last directions to her servants.				
			SCENE IV
A new scene for Demon-Merchants and Peasants on their way to the market [18 lines, excluding S.D.s].	SCENE IV *A
Demon-Merchants re-placed by song for Aleel ('Impetuous heart, be still, be still').
SCENES IV & V *A
SCENE IV: Merchants and Peasants traffic in souls; Kevin attempts to sell his soul but it is refused; the Countess enters and sells her soul; the scene ends with the triumphant disappearance of the Merchants ('Leap, feathered, on the air . . .').

SCENE V: Oona's vision. | ACT III *A

(No scene-division.)

Completely re-written as Aleel's vision. | ACT IV *A

[Modified for 1911 revival.] | SCENE V *A | SCENE V *A |

I thought, a dramatic vehicle. The tumultuous and heroic Pagan cycle, on the other hand, having to do with vast and shadowy activities and with the great impersonal emotions, expressed itself naturally—or so I imagined—in epic and epic-lyric measures. No epic method seemed sufficiently minute and subtle for the one, and no dramatic method elastic and all-containing enough for the other.[10]

The writing and thinking here seem clumsy, but Yeats did not lightly abandon anything having to do with *The Countess Cathleen*, a play which gave him 'more pleasure in the memory than any of my plays'.[11] The cumbrous distinctions of the 1892 Preface took fire nearly half a century later in the majestic lines of 'The Circus Animals' Desertion':

> What can I but enumerate old themes?
> First that sea-rider Oisin led by the nose
> Through three enchanted islands, allegorical dreams,
> Vain gaiety, vain battle, vain repose,
> Themes of the embittered heart, or so it seems,
> That might adorn old songs and courtly shows;
> But what cared I that set him on to ride,
> I, starved for the bosom of his faery bride?
>
> And then a counter-truth filled out its play,
> *The Countess Cathleen* was the name I gave it. . . .[12]

The play, then, at its earliest stage was to be dramatic, not epic-lyric, Christian, not Pagan, and was to deal with subtle actions and personal and moral emotions. Here a second influence on its design needs to be taken into account. 'He started', writes Mr. Henn, speaking of the year 1889, '*The Countess Cathleen* . . . the first projection of his own love and despair.'[13] Yeats in 1938 would have agreed with him, for the stanza in 'The Circus Animals' Desertion' continues:

> *The Countess Cathleen* was the name I gave it;
> She, pity-crazed, had given her soul away,
> But masterful Heaven had intervened to save it.
> I thought my dear must her own soul destroy,
> So did fanaticism and hate enslave it. . . .

Hone, too, writes, dating the incident in 1891, that Yeats read to Maud Gonne 'his unpublished *Countess Cathleen* and told her that

16

she had come to interpret the life of a woman who sells her soul a
a symbol of all souls that lose their peace, their fineness in politics,
serving but change'.[14] It is true that Maud Gonne, whom Yeats
met for the first time on January 30, 1889, shortly after the
publication of *The Wanderings of Oisin*, was very much present in
his mind when the play was begun in March. She was perhaps the
unnamed 'actress' to whom on May 6, 1889, as Yeats told John
O'Leary the following day, he read 'a scene' of the new work:
'She seemed to think it suitable in all ways for the stage. I think
you will like it. It is in all things Celtic and Irish. The style is
perfectly simple and I have taken great care with the construction,
made two complete prose versions before writing a line of
verse.'[15] Much later, according to Maud Gonne, he was still
hoping that she would play the part:

That evening Willie Yeats was sad and tried hard to persuade me to
act the part of Countess Kathleen. 'I wrote it for you and if you don't
act it we shall have to get an actress from London to take the part',
which eventually he did, with no marked success.[16]

The dedication of 1892 went even further: '. . . To My Friend,
Miss Maud Gonne, At whose Suggestion It was Planned out and
Begun. . . .' The statement, though, conflicts with an earlier one,
made in another letter to John O'Leary on February 1, 1889, that
he had 'long been intending to write [a poetic drama with a view
to the stage] founded on the tale of "Countess Kathleen O'Shea"
in the folk lore book'.[17]

The difficulty about accepting Henn's or Hone's or Yeats's own
interpretations (whether of 1891 or 1938) simply as they stand is
that none of the versions of *The Countess Cathleen* offers us a protagonist whose selling of her soul can possibly be interpreted as self-
destruction through fanaticism or hate; nor can the Countess's
bargain, in its context, be easily read as a symbol of the loss of
peace and fineness through political activity. Whatever the part
played by 'personal thought and feeling', as developed in Yeats's
relation to Maud Gonne, in *The Countess Cathleen*, it was much less
forthright than 'The Circus Animals' Desertion' suggests and
much more gradually infiltrated into successive versions than the
story of the play's origin between 1889 and 1891 at first sight
implies. Had the play resembled its description in the poem more

closely it might have proved a more powerful and lasting work. Had the 'personal thought and feeling' been accorded franker recognition in the text from the beginning, instead of gaining admission to it by stages, it might have been an altogether better piece of architecture. And the 'soul-making' Yeats of the later period may well have permitted his repugnance at the idea of anyone's actually giving her soul away 'under any circumstances' to blind him to what he had written.

III

A comparison of the 1892 version with its source makes some things clear. Yeats adopts most of its details with some significant changes of direction: the appearance of the demon-merchants in the poverty-stricken land, their ostentatious display of wealth, Ketty O'Donnor's decision to save the peasants by selling all her treasure, and the consequent frustration of the demons, who decide, therefore, to rob her:

Aidés par un valet infâme, ils pénétrèrent dans la retraite de la noble dame et lui dérobèrent le reste de son trésor . . . en vain lutta-t-elle de toutes ses forces pour sauver le contenu de son coffre, les larrons diaboliques furent les plus forts. Si Ketty avait eu les moyens de faire un signe de croix, ajoute la légende irlandaise, elle les eût mis en fuite, mais ses mains étaient captive—Le larcin fut effectué.[18]

The Countess has no resource left but to sell her own soul for the highest price she can get.

The powerful and self-consistent structure of this fable is present in Yeats's play but the weight of scene and incident rests only lightly upon it. Thus, the passage which has just been quoted seems to provide an obvious opportunity for a dramatist. Even if the rendering of the conflict with the demons as the physical struggle implied in the source might have appeared too external a way of treating it, the plot seems to call here for some surge of the protagonist's will against demonic outrage. Instead, the Countess remains passively in her oratory while the merchants rob her treasure-house, nor does she discover her loss and their identity until after they have fled the scene. The robbery-scene itself, as preserved through several re-writings until it is virtually eliminated after 1912, is an elaborate affair during which the water-spirits and lost souls (sheogues, tevishies, and sowlths— there are variant spellings) carry away the bags of treasure under the compulsion of the demons. That this kind of thing should be substituted for the more direct encounter with the Countess (and that that suggestive figure the 'valet infâme' should disappear altogether) is in part a concession to Yeats's desire to make his drama 'in all things Celtic and Irish'. This was undoubtedly one of the factors that influenced his treatment of his source.

But, perhaps more important, the Countess's altered role here points directly at an element in the play for which Yeats had no warrant in his source. The original story stresses conflict between the saint and the demonic powers. It was open to Yeats to drama- tize this as an outward and inward struggle in and for the soul and body of his protagonist, and in particular to represent her final decision to sacrifice her soul as the outcome of a profound and agonizing προαίρεσις. This is what the critics of the play were dis- mayed to find largely missing from it. Yeats must have known what was said by the first man to write a book about him, who affirmed in 1904, with (presumably) the version of 1901 in mind, that there was

no obstinate struggle of opposing notions in the soul of Cathleen her- self, and no stirring dramatic conflict between the forces of good and evil. . . . The dramatic knot is tied and untied in the simplest way . . . the climax scene is not made the most of dramatically.[19]

But this criticism misses the point in so far as it fails to observe how Yeats was deliberately re-shaping his material. For his Countess the interior conflict is not between the need to sacrifice and the desire to save her soul; her trouble begins at an earlier stage. It has to do with the war between dreams and responsi- bility, between the land of pagan images of Fergus and Adene, Usheen, young Neave and the Fenians on one side and the 'burden of the world's wrongs', the famine, and the starving peasantry on the other. It is in this sense that *The Countess Cathleen* is a 'counter- truth' to *The Wanderings of Oisin*. In that poem Oisin finally chooses the Fenians and rejects St. Patrick; in the play the Countess reverses this choice. In the 1892 version her reluctance to do this is rendered in Scene ii:

19

O, I am sadder than an old air, Oona,
My heart is longing for a deeper peace
Than Fergus found amid his brazen cars:
Would that like Adene my first forebear's daughter
Who followed once a twilight piercing tune,
I could go down and dwell among the Shee
In their old ever-busy honeyed land.

But her peace is interrupted three times: by the Gardener with his news of pillaged orchards, by the Herdsman with his news of stolen sheep, and finally by the peasants with their news of the Mephistophelean bargaining. When once her peace has been destroyed by this last manifest claim for succour, such 'struggle of opposing notions' as is allowed for by the design is over. Her charity takes a plain course and surmounts the ultimate test of it; we hear no more about that in herself which alone could have made it falter—the longing for, in Oona's words in the 1895 version, 'a soft cradle of old tales, And songs, and music'. The dramatist interprets his task, after her first and last renunciation has been made, as simply to render as veraciously and spiritedly as possible the tale of the demon-merchants and how they are finally cheated of the Countess's soul.

This is unexpected, but it has a pace and logic of its own. It is the element in the play which is most easily to be identified with the 'personal thought and feeling' mentioned in the 1892 Preface. Flight into the artifice of dream 'under quiet boughs apart' is a constant theme of the lyrics in the volumes of 1889 and 1892. There is little reason to suppose that the first version of Cathleen would have been any different had Yeats and Maud Gonne never met. For what the Countess there embodies is thematic material which had already found expression in the lyrics. If she is to be identified with anyone it is with those fictive voices rather than with a living woman.

But with later versions it is another matter. Yeats had begun by introducing an emphasis alien to his source and by refusing suggestions that might have appealed to a dramatist less concerned with the personal and the subtle. It was this re-making of the 'conflict between the forces of good and evil' into a hinted choice between dreams and responsibility that was to grow progressively into a much more elaborate structure. It changed and expanded until it can fairly be said that some symbolic adumbration of Yeats's notions about Maud Gonne and about beautiful women who betray themselves by climbing on wagonettes to scream can, by the eye of faith, be discerned in it. It can at least be said that the Countess, who began as a *persona*, in some degree, of Yeats himself, began to look much more like a heroic mask modelled from Maud Gonne's noble lineaments. But for the critic of the play this is not the primary issue: his task is rather to decide whether the new growth didn't mortally injure the old tale. Its roots begin to split the old foundation, like those of a tree growing upon a ruin. Did the foundations, already rendered dramatically less robust than they might have been, simply crack, and bring themselves and their parasite down in mutual disorder?

IV

The new element, as it expanded, did not mean that Yeats simply yielded to an appetite for what bore upon 'personal thought and feeling' without regard for his structure as a whole and for the needs of the theatre as he came to understand them better. The changes in 1895, indeed, attempt chiefly to devise a better final scene and a more efficient narrative.

The entry of the Countess, Aleel, and the Musicians in Act I was written into the 1895 version. This episode was retained in all subsequent versions, although it was entirely re-drafted along with the rest of the Act in 1912. While it does not tell us very much about the new characters, and while the necessity which it imposes upon the Countess to call on one of her cottagers in order to find the way to her own Castle is a trifle grotesque, the episode can be justified in two ways. The difference between them provides an insight into the curious economies practised by Yeats in the work of revising. On one level, the entry of the Countess and her crowd of 'fantastically dressed musicians' into the hunger-bitten cottage, her charity (ineffective), and Aleel's lyrical insouciance, as well as the whole pictorial stage-contrast between real rags and gorgeous livery, foreshadow what is later to be the Countess's choice: retreat into the artifice of fable or acknowledgement of a land where people die of hunger, their mouths 'green with dock and dandelion'. Here is an early example of the handling of counter-truths of which Yeats never wearied. On another level, it must have seemed an advantage to introduce the Countess at an earlier stage than the opening of the second Act. This risked break-ing up the action that, in the 1892 version, leads straight from starvation-induced despair to the entry of the demon-merchants; a parable, complete in itself, about the irruption of supernatural evil into the heart and hearth. But Yeats apparently preferred to interweave his first and second Acts more efficiently at the cost of losing some sharpness of effect within the first Act itself. This cannot have been his only motive for the alteration. For this new episode is also related to the new ending of the 1895 version of the play.

Scene v in 1892 concludes with Oona's vision of the angelic spirits. In 1895 this was transformed into the far more elaborate war-in-heaven and apotheosis, and these are mediated to us not by Oona but by Aleel. As the 1895 version stands, the only previous appearance of Aleel before the last Act was in the new episode of the first Act. His place there is justified because it would never have done for Aleel to be introduced to us for the first time at the end of the play, since curiosity about this new personage would have deflected our attention from the visionary scenes of which he is the agent and interpreter. As, in versions after 1895, the part of Aleel is expanded still further and he appears in more and more scenes, this argument in defence of the new episode in Act I becomes much less cogent. By 1901 we have already seen quite enough of Aleel in the earlier part of the play to accept him as the visionary of the last Act without wondering how he comes to be there at all or who he is. Yeats could have afforded, so far as the coherence of his narrative was in question, to eliminate in later versions the new episode in Act I and give back to the Act the driving unity and sinister logic that make the 1892 version of it structurally better than any of the later ones. This is an example of a feature which seems at one stage of the revision to be accept-able and necessary, but at another to become, in the course of the play's evolution, something that we could do without.

The new ending of 1895 was, apart from a few minor changes, retained in all subsequent versions. In so far as it gratifies expecta-tion by giving the Countess a death-bed and not just a funeral, it is undoubtedly more effective than the final scene was in 1892.

But in lyrical elaboration, mythological allusions, and scenic effects it far surpasses anything in the earliest version, and moves away from simplicity and 'masculinity'. Just as does the new episode in Act I, with its pictorial contrast between rags and splendour, so this scene, with its knightly angels 'as impossibly tall as one of those figures at Chartres Cathedral',[20] reminds us of Arthur Symons's belief, shared by Yeats,[21] that

If we take drama with any seriousness, as an art as well as an improvisation, we shall realize that one of its main requirements is that it should make pictures.[22]

All this proved too much for the stage at Yeats's disposal. For the revival of 1911 he was forced to produce something less elaborate.[23] And although Lennox Robinson thought well of it,[24] the result seems timid and constrained, simplified rather than simple, and marked by concessions of which John O'Leary would have disapproved, such as the substitution of Belial for Balor. Yeats did not print this more practical solution in his text, but relegated it to an appendix. Why did he not go back, at least for theatrical purposes, to the version of 1892? It has certain virtues, even though the speeches of the Angel about the Countess's acceptance into heaven have not yet attained their classic form. There is much to be said, so far as dramatic suggestion goes, for the way Oona finds the owl-feathers of the demons scattered upon the steps of the oratory:

some bird,
Some hawk or kestrel, chased its prey to this.

This conveys, with suggestive brevity, the war between demon and angel upon which, in the later versions, Aleel's speeches insist with something of the 'strained lyricism' that Yeats found so objectionable in Morris. But in 1911 Yeats could not go back to the 1892 version and to Oona's vision because by then Aleel had become too important in the body of the play for him not to have his place at the end of it. Here again the expansion of one element in the course of the revisions has to some extent tied Yeats's hands as a theatrical craftsman and forced him to write for the stage something he could not bring himself to print in the received text. The writing of a 'stage version' and a 'reading version' was a solution Yeats adopted on other occasions as well; but in this case it is an admission of failure as a dramatic poet.

The continuous enlargement of Aleel's role is of course the most striking feature of all the revised versions. In 1892 he makes (under the name Kevin) a momentary appearance in Scene iv, and tries to sell his soul to the merchants, and, a little later in the scene, he tries to prevent the Countess selling hers:

> You shall yet know the love of some great chief,
> And children gathering round your knees. Leave you
> The peasants to the builder of the heavens.

Out of these hints Yeats gradually developed the part. He added his entry with Cathleen in Act I and his vision in Act III (1895), the love-scene with Cathleen in Act III (1901), another similar scene in Scene iii (1912), until eventually in the final version there is no single scene of the five in which he does not appear. The impulse behind this enlargement was certainly autobiographical. Aleel now speaks for Yeats himself and is the chief means by which the element of 'personal thought and feeling' achieves progressively fuller expression. What was, in the versions of 1892 and 1895, simply the Countess's vain longing for a peace breathed forth by Oona's tales of 'the Danaan nations in their raths' becomes in the third version objectified in the relation with Aleel. As poet, dreamer, and lover, urging her retirement to the Druid forest, to the subjective life of peaceful beauty away from the objective life of self-sacrifice and war, Aleel has many links with Yeats's later verse. The invention and development of Aleel's and Cathleen's duologue is also Yeats's way of contriving a more theatrical and more deeply personal method for representing the old quarrel between St. Patrick and the Fenians, or 'dreaming' and 'grey Truth'.

In expanding this element Yeats was doing no more than submit to the logical consequences of his first departure from his source. Already, when the Countess listens to Oona's tales and songs, the possibility of a choice between dream and action, self-absorption and self-sacrifice, her own 'good' and her own 'evil', is hinted at. The scheme of the play, which shows her final sacrifice as an act of uncomplicated exaltation, seems to suggest that once she has made the sacrifice of the self entailed upon her by taking action at all, all other sacrifices, even the surrender of her soul, unresistedly ensue. In the revisions of 1901 and 1912 Yeats was moving nearer and nearer to a pattern of this kind.

Thus it is significant that nowhere in the revision does he attempt to lay any greater emphasis than he had in 1892 on what in the source is the natural dramatic climax of the fable: Cathleen's offer of her soul. And Aleel himself finally becomes, in the last version, a complete and successful symbol of the subjective life, messenger of Aedh and Aengus, bearer of the 'unchristened heart'. From the moment when he is first heard of, wandering and singing on the border of the woods 'wrapped up in dreams of terrors to come', until his last vision of Cathleen's transfiguration 'smitten of God' he serves to convey more richly than anything in the 1892 and 1895 versions what was written in the Yeatsian 'books of numberless dreams': he foreshadows Paul Ruttledge in *Where There is Nothing*, Septimus in *The Player Queen*, the author of 'The Second Coming' and even perhaps Ribh himself. The Aleel scenes, also, by the kind of contrast they make with the rest of the play, help to outline this pattern. The love scene in Act III (added in 1901) and the episode before the Castle in Scene ii (added in 1912), like the passages for Oona and Cathleen which it replaces, are slow-paced, lyrical, and evocatively full of pagan imagery. They do indeed turn aside 'at the lure of word and metaphor' because such turning-aside is appropriate to Aleel's role as the poet who repudiates the 'day's war' with the demons and 'all things uncomely and broken'.[25] The scenes strive to be timeless moments of suspended action:

> I thought to have kept her from remembering
> The evil of the times for full ten minutes.

Each is deliberately juxtaposed to other scenes that rapidly forward the perturbations of the play as it advances towards the demonic bargain: the arrival of Teig and Shemus with their gold, which moves the Countess to expend her treasure for the salvation of her people; and the robbery, leading to the Countess's 'stern resolve' and farewell to her hope of heaven. Christian images are plentifully scattered here. These contrasts of time's speed with time's suspension, of lyrical meditation with dramatic event, and of mythology with piety, actualize Cathleen's two worlds and underline in a substantially theatrical way the opposition between them.

Yeats thus gradually makes us alive to his pattern of counter-truths. In the original fable the stress was all on the Countess's desperate, physical struggle; in the first version this struggle, translated into the war between dreams and responsibility, still took place, so far as it is recognized at all, chiefly in Cathleen's soul. In later versions the divergent truths achieve greater theatrical life, but it is embodied in the antithesis between Cathleen and Aleel, two dramatic characters. The difference shows Yeats's movement towards a theatrical strategy and away from dependence upon a protagonist too close to the speaker of his lyrics, who does not really need for the expression of his nature the relationships with other people for which drama asks. It is true, however, that no struggle between self and soul, objective and subjective, in the single personality of Cathleen occurs. In the scenes with Aleel the Countess has little to do except to bring out *his* symbolic status. His is a story and a sorrow which does not touch her except with pity. It is never admitted to her imagination as a temptation which, by awakening a response in the depth of her own nature, can weaken her resolve or make her actions in other episodes appear as the issue of the soul's triumph over the self. We do not see in her what Yeats called 'the two halves of the soul separate and face to face'.[26] This is because Yeats is trying to show, in Cathleen and Aleel, what he was later to call Artist and Saint confronting each other upon the stage. We may prefer to think (as Yeats often did) of Self and Soul, or Artist and Saint, as more finely conceived when they are rendered as two contradictory elements in the same personality; and so we may criticize *The Countess Cathleen* for being too pale a version of a struggle that, partly because it is confined within the bounds of a single lyric life, seems so much more intense in such poems as 'The Choice' or 'Vacillation' or 'A Dialogue of Self and Soul'. Or we may prefer to argue that the fable which Yeats had chosen was not well adapted to the increasingly autobiographical use to which he put it; that the story of Ketty O'Donnor cannot really be made to fit what grew, as the play evolved, into the portrait of the artist as the rejected lover of Maud Gonne. These would, indeed, be valid criticisms, and there may underlie them the deeper recognition that both Cathleen

26

and Aleel demonstrate an ever simpler and more schematic method of characterization—each the 'half' rather than the whole of a personality. But these criticisms ought not to obscure the extent to which Yeats's use of autobiography—the recognition that two persons are involved—actually supported the theatrical strategy—the recognition that a play is not a single lyric voice.

Elsewhere in the last two revisions Yeats's object was to tighten rather than to expand his construction. The most striking example of this is what happens to the robbery-scene from the going-out of the Countess until her re-entry to discourse with the merchants. In the first three versions this is very elaborately rendered and filled with Celtic colour and local pieties, such as the story of how the demons killed the good priest but could not entrap his soul. It dwells much also upon the nature and ambience of the demons themselves. In 1912 the scene, which had constantly attracted a good deal of minor tinkering, was completely re-written in a much compressed form, with only one set of servant-spirits. They are now supplied with lyric chants of a vapidity astonishing at this stage of Yeats's development. In the final version this re-writing was scrapped, leaving only half a dozen lines and a few stage directions.

Yeats judged soundly in other ways too. The complete revision of Scenes i and ii, accomplished in 1912, while it scarcely alters a single one of the old incidents and retains (with the exception of the new scene for Cathleen and Aleel in Scene ii) the episodes in their old order, makes both Scenes much tougher and faster. Scene ii, for example, had remained virtually unaltered since 1892, except for minor adjustments and the re-writing of two or three lines here and there. When he re-wrote it Yeats made the incidents seem much more urgent, economized on characters, and improved narrative articulation. Thus it is Teig and Shemus, characters already introduced in the first Act, and not a couple of anonymous peasants who convince Cathleen of the true nature of the evil that is abroad by showing her their infernal gold. An anxious steward brings news of the thieving and disorder in the demesne, whereas in the previous versions a Gardener and a Herdsman occupy two long passages by somewhat repetitiously conveying the same point. Similar adjustments, on a smaller scale, are found elsewhere, such as the passage added in 1912 preceding

27

the Countess's entry in Scene v, when the peasants are panicked by the old woman's scream of hellish pain and try to revoke their bargains. This adds spirit and movement to the moment of Cathleen's arrival, which is slack and undramatic in earlier versions.

Throughout the revision Yeats sedulously watches out for the worst archaisms in modes of address and speech, gradually eliminates the more self-conscious spots of local colour and the weaker and more automatic lapses into Jacobean rhythms. Much of this work, in those parts of the play which were not completely re-written in the last two versions, had already been done by 1895. Especially in the last scene the more famous speeches had by then attained a form with which Yeats was apparently reluctant to meddle. Yet he did sometimes do so, and in making them swifter and sparer eliminated some beauty as well as some non-sense. This is the first form of a well-known passage:

> *First Merchant.* Five hundred thousand crowns—we give the price,
> The gold is here—the spirits, while you speak,
> Begin to labour upward, for your face
> Sheds a great light on them and fills their hearts
> With those unveilings of the fickle light,
> Whereby our heavy labours have been marred
> Since first His spirit moved upon the deeps
> And stole them from us. Even before this day
> The souls were but half ours, for your bright eyes
> Had pierced them through and robbed them of content.
> But you must sign, for we do all in order
> In buying such a soul—sign with this quill;
> It was a feather growing on the cock
> That crowed when Peter had denied his Master;
> 'Tis a great honour thus to write with it.[27]

In 1895 the end of this speech, which was otherwise untouched, attained the classic form which caused such concern to Dublin defenders of the papal honour:

> But you must sign, for we omit no form
> In buying a soul like yours; sign with this quill;
> It was a feather growing on the cock
> That crowed when Peter dared deny his Master,
> And all who use it have great honour in hell.

But the last version of all reads:

First Merchant. Five hundred thousand crowns; we give the price.
The gold is here; the souls even while you speak
Have slipped out of our bond, because your face
Has shed a light on them and filled their hearts.
But you must sign, for we omit no form
In buying a soul like yours. Sign with this quill.
Second Merchant. It was a feather growing on the cock
That crowed when Peter dared deny his Master,
And all who use it have great honour in Hell.

The Fay brothers would have found the last version easier to speak on the stage. A preference for the intermediate version would have to meet the objections that the metaphors about 'light' seem irrelated and that a damned soul could hardly become less damned through being discontented.

These alterations are not of the sort that affect construction or change the kind of play *The Countess Cathleen* is. Throughout the thirty years' history of revision Yeats remained substantially faithful to the design which he had described to John O'Leary. If the play does not quite give us the sense of being 'laboriously constructed scene by scene', it is devised episode by episode. Yeats continued to work with these small units in all his revisions, re-handling them, or intercalating them with fresh ones on the same scale. But these new episodes—especially the two Aleel scenes of 1901 and 1912—are not out of quite the same box as the old ones. They hint at another kind of play, one which consists not of episodes linked together but of a single episode explored in depths. The story of Aleel and Cathleen moves towards such a design, but, because it is rooted in a play conceived as a cumulative succession of episodes, does not achieve it.

Amongst the plays of the Abbey Theatre period there are two which develop these contrasting principles in a specially instructive way. *The King's Threshold* is once more fashioned out of many units but they 'grow, or are wrought, together', in Ben Jonson's phrase, much better. *Deirdre*, on the other hand, is a more perfect example than *The Shadowy Waters* of a play of the other kind, a single episode more deeply explored. *Deirdre*, of all the earlier

29

plays, has most bearing on Yeats's future as a playwright. But the curious history of *The Countess Cathleen* perhaps permitted him to observe that there were, at the least, two kinds of play for him to write, and even, as *The King's Threshold* suggests, that he could have another try at writing both kinds at once.

Chapter Two

The Man that Dies

THE KING'S THRESHOLD

I

THE difference between Aleel, the dreamer of the Pre-Raphaelite Twilight, and Seanchan, the obdurate professional of *The King's Threshold*, signalizes a well-attested shift in Yeats's interpretation of his own role as a poet in society. But *The King's Threshold* is, in the best sense, an amateur play, and almost the last play by Yeats of which this could properly be said. Unexacting in its staging and lucid in the development of its theme, it has many small parts which need only to be played with vigour and conviction to be brought to life. Yeats was later to group it with *Deirdre* and *On Baile's Strand*. Each, he thought, wanted 'one player of genius and that is out of reach probably henceforth for ever'.[1] But the difference between Seanchan and Deirdre is more justly apprehended if we remember that Frank Fay played the one part, and Mrs. Patrick Campbell the other. Earlier, Yeats had coupled the play with *The Countess Cathleen* as

easier to play effectively than my later plays, depending less upon the players and more upon the producer, both having been imagined more for variety of stage-picture than variety of mood in the player.[2]

The stage-pictures are composed by the entries of such contrasting figures as the pupils, the Mayor of Kinvara, the cripples, the monk,

31

the princesses. The construction, 'rather like a Greek play',[3] is controlled by their mutual purpose, which is to persuade Seanchan the Chief Poet to abandon his fast against the indignity that Guaire, King of Gort, has inflicted upon poetry by dismissing him from his place at the council-table. An action which consists of a series of short episodes, or temptations, is unified in place and time. The play dramatizes the last hour of the dying poet and the shame or glory which his triumph or death bestow upon Guaire's threshold; the threshold where Seanchan lies is the emblem of that in the royal condition which is capable of knowing honour and dishonour.

This element of variety within unity in the design of the play will influence a critical judgement upon it. It is an advance on *The Countess Cathleen*, where the episodes tend to fall apart and string themselves out among distracting counter-movements. The sources, too, reveal something about how the play was made: the *Immtheacht na Tromdáimhe*[4] is a good deal less important than Edwin Ellis's obscure and rubbishy verse-play *Sancan the Bard* (1895), to which Yeats acknowledged his indebtedness for 'arrangements' when the first version of *The King's Threshold* was printed in 1904.[5]

Edwin Ellis was not interested in making a play that could be put on the stage, but hankers after that continuous lyricism for which some of Yeats's earlier critics pleaded, in their dismay at the buffoonery in *The King's Threshold* and *On Baile's Strand* and at the baldness of the language of *Deirdre*.[6] Because his hero was a poet, Ellis crammed his play, which is written in rhyming couplets, with bad poems, specimens of the art that Sancan is upholding; Yeats was too skilful to endanger our belief in the Chief Poet in that way. Perhaps the most marked difference in method between Ellis and Yeats was Yeats's care to localize his drama. The principle, which is hardly operative in *The Countess Cathleen*, and is necessarily absent from the other-worldly ocean of *The Shadowy Waters*, had been determinedly applied in *On Baile's Strand* and was enunciated a few years before that play was written:

Our legends are always associated with places, and not merely every mountain and valley, but every strange stone and little coppice, has its legend, preserved in written or unwritten tradition. Our Irish romantic movement has arisen out of this tradition, and should always, even when it makes new legends about traditional people and things, be haunted by places.[7]

Once established, the principle was never forgotten; it was its sense of place that counted as one of the attractions of the Noh. In *The King's Threshold*, whereas Ellis was content to leave everything vague, Yeats sets his scene in Gort, of which Guaire is King, Seanchan is a citizen of Kinvara, and there are abounding references to the Clare-Galway landscape, as well as to hurley, salt fish, cranes, cripples, stony meadows and crooked thorn-trees.

Yet, despite these differences, the play owes much to *Sancan the Bard*. Ellis, like Yeats, devised a series of episodes in which various persons try to divert the martyr's purpose; they include the King, a Courtier, a Princess (and her attendant), and one of Sancan's pupils. Yeats added the Mayor of Kinvara, Seanchan's faithful servant (in the first version there are two of them), a Monk, and a Soldier. Seanchan's betrothed Fedelm in Yeats's play is, however, a radically different character from the Girl in Ellis's, who is a 'tribal maid' captured in battle and ordered by the King to persuade Sancan to eat under penalty of being burnt at the stake if she fails. *Sancan the Bard* ends with the mysterious love which Sancan and the Girl discover for each other: as singer and lover, each actualizes the other's ideal. Their determination to perish together causes the King to relent, while a Chorus of Bards proclaims a general reconciliation. Yeats, who had temporarily exhausted this *Axel*-like theme in *The Shadowy Waters* put nothing of it into *The King's Threshold*, but, apart from the general debt which his construction owes to Ellis, he borrowed other details from his work. An example is Seanchan's speech about the leprous beggar, which so horrifies the Princess, and which derives from a passage in Scene iv of *Sancan the Bard*:

> Long years ago I saw thy granddam, girl:
> She sat upon a bank one summer's day,
> Then came three lepers asking her the way.
> She told them, and her hand she waved and showed;
> The lepers saw, and passed upon the road.
> Your hand has still some evil taint of this.

It will be seen that *Sancan the Bard* ends not with the death of the poet but with the repeal of the ordinance that had banished him from his place amongst the makers of the law at the king's table. In the received text of *The King's Threshold*, of course, this is not so. At the end of the play Seanchan dies and is carried to his mountain-tomb far from the 'worsening world'. Yeats's sense that 'the man that dies has the chief part in the story' did not become clear until the play had undergone two revisions. In both the versions which precede the final one (which was done in 1922 and first printed in *Plays in Prose and Verse Written for an Irish Theatre*) the play ends with the happy restoration of the poet's right, as Guaire kneels before him and accepts his crown from his hands.

The revisions of *The King's Threshold* tell a simpler story than those of *The Countess Cathleen*, but the two stories have some common features. The first version, printed in 1904, did not last very long before about two-thirds of it were thoroughly re-written as printed in *Poems 1899–1905* (1906).* A comparison of these two versions of 1904 and 1906—for they may be spoken of as two, although there are a great number of minor differences between the various printings of the second version—shows how skilful Yeats had become, once he had seen a play of his performed, in making better theatre out of it. A few examples are enough, for the operations are of the same kind as those carried out for those parts of *The Countess Cathleen* where the introduction of new thematic material is not in question.

It is plainly less tiresome for the audience to listen to Guaire's expository speech near the beginning of the play in its new form—broken up by interruptions from the Pupil—than in its

* The 1904 version was printed privately at New York (Wade No. 55) and in Volume III of *Plays for an Irish Theatre*; identical with this is a Dublin edition of 1905 (Volume V of the 'Abbey Theatre Series'). The 1906 version is substantially that found in all reprintings before 1922, but there are slight differences between these reprintings as they appear successively in *Poems 1899–1905*, *The Poetical Works of William B. Yeats* Volume II (New York, 1907), *Collected Works* Volume II (Stratford-on-Avon, 1908), and *Plays for an Irish Theatre* (London and Stratford-on-Avon, 1911). This last edition restores to the text the long prose-prologue which furnished forth the play in the editions of 1904 and 1905, but the prologue disappeared again in the final (third) version in *Plays in Prose and Verse Written for an Irish Theatre* (1922). The author's note on performance and revision, misleadingly dated 1911, in the 1922 edition is a shortened form of a similar note which first appeared in *Poems 1899–1905* (1906).

first form, where it continues without change of direction for nearly fifty lines. There is far more interplay between the subsidiary characters, as in the new passage where the Chamberlain fails, but the girls with their blandishments succeed in persuading the reluctant Soldier to tempt Seanchan with the food. The Monk is handled in much the same way, and given more satirical vitality by a speech against the music and dancing that the court-ladies have been deprived of by Seanchan's strike. The Fedelm episode towards the end of the play bites deeper because the cross-purposes in which the lovers are entangled break, in the second version, into a bitter quarrel. This sharpening of the relations between the characters has the general effect of clarifying the issue between Seanchan as the transcendent poet and all the other personages, who stand by Church, by State, by pleasure, or by love. The episode most radically affected by this process is the visit of the Mayor of Kinvara. He, of course, is deplorably bourgeois and low in the first version, but comically so in the second, and a renegade as well; he is the true voice of the 'blind and ignorant town', of the greedy and sycophantic philistinism which Yeats attacked in the poems in *Responsibilities*. Indeed, in the second version he becomes almost too complex a figure, for we may suspect Lady Gregory's hand in the cosy comedy of his half-remembered speech,* and Yeats's in the fresh virulence with which the Cripples now rhyme him from the door and the Chamberlain pushes him, a turncoat and flatterer, off the stage.

All such changes light up more effectively those 'stage-pictures' which, as they are revealed in successive episodes, compose the outward theatrical 'busyness' of the play; they also underline the theme of the society which mistakes just pride for arrogant assertion. As Yeats himself observed, the play was not changed 'in the radical structure' [8] in 1906, and the revision simply brings to fuller life what was already there. He found Ellis's original

---

* We can only speculate about how much Lady Gregory helped. The play's debt to *Sancan the Bard* makes it probable that the original plan was Yeats's, since he would have been the first to get to know of the work of a friend and co-editor. Lady Gregory writes: 'For *The Pot of Broth* I wrote dialogue and I worked as well at the plot and construction of some of the poetic plays, especially *The King's Threshold* and *Deirdre*; for I had learned by this time a good deal about playwriting to which I had never given a thought before' (*Our Irish Theatre*, New York, 1914, pp. 82–3).

structure adequate for embodying a vision of Seanchan and his martyrdom which was much nearer to Swift and Shaw than to Ellis's rhapsodies about love and fate.

The sharper colour, because it is new, has called attention to itself; but it ought not to be overstressed when the play as a whole is thought about. What Una Ellis-Fermor described as 'the apocalyptic vision of the function of poetry' [9] is brilliant in the first version and undiminished in the second and third. It was to be some time before the more sardonic eye that he was now in 1906 turning upon the poet's town took in the poet himself and transformed *him* into an 'old scarecrow'.[10] But this, too, was to happen, and it is Yeats himself who has made it difficult for us to accept sentiment or idiom in such a speech as

> O silver trumpets be you lifted up
> And cry to the great race that is to come. . . .

The quieter and less exalted passages carry more conviction, such as the Pupil's image of a world without art as

> like a woman
> That looking on the cloven lips of a hare
> Brings forth a hare-lipped child

or Seanchan's reply to the Soldier's 'Eat this, old hedge-hog'. This is a fine example of dramatic speech, tied to its context, and conveying the movement of the speaker as his mind turns away in self-contemplation from his interlocutor and then back again in vivid indignation as the angry pride rises:

> You have rightly named me.
> I lie rolled up under the ragged thorns
> That are upon the edge of those great waters
> Where all things vanish away, and I have heard
> Murmurs that are the ending of all sound.
> I am out of life, I am rolled up, and yet
> Hedgehog although I am, I'll not unroll
> For you, King's dog. Go to the King, your master. . .

But these excellent inventions of the first version are all the better for the more generally efficient context which the second provides for them.

Yet even this version must always have been regarded by Yeats as an unsatisfying compromise. It was not until the third and final version that Yeats gave the play the 'tragic end I would have given it at the first, had not a friend advised me to "write comedy and have a few happy moments in the theatre" '.[11] The earlier part of the 1922 text differs here and there only in minor ways from the 1906 version; but the play has a quite new ending, a passage of some sixty lines (incorporating the old 'O silver trumpets' speech which Yeats could not bear to abandon); it begins after the Youngest Pupil's 'Die, Seanchan . . .' with Seanchan's dying speech ('Come nearer me . . .').[12]

This type of alteration is one that is bound to arouse suspicion about the integrity of any of the versions. If the last episode in a play made up of a series of episodes can be so utterly transformed, could not the celebrated objection that Dr. Johnson brought against that other 'Greek' play, Samson Agonistes, be brought against the construction of this one, that 'the intermediate parts have neither cause nor consequence, neither hasten nor retard the catastrophe'?

I think it can be shown that the violence was done to the two earlier versions rather than to the last, and that it is they which bear the scars. Nothing in the various episodes enforces a happy ending. Each, even the climactic one of the temptation by Fedelm, terminates in Seanchan's remaining irremovably staunch. This lays it down plainly enough that, if anyone is to yield, Guaire must do so. Yet everything we are told about Guaire's dilemma suggests that it has been carefully contrived to prevent his escape from it by any mere change of heart. If Seanchan dies, Guaire's house will be shamed; but if he restores the poet's right, his throne will be in danger. Apart from this dilemma and his masterful impatience at being faced with it, we are told very little about Guaire. This does not help us to believe in his final reversal of his decision. We cannot explain his change, since the pressures upon him have not apparently been in any way modified in the course of the play's action, nor are we vouchsafed any explanation of it in terms of movements in Guaire's own mind. In the first version Yeats, with some dexterity, succeeds in keeping these worries mostly dormant by bringing the curtain down before we have had time to think about them, and bringing it down on a scene of melodrama—the Pupils with halters round their necks, their

37

last-ditch defiance in defence of the ancient right, and Guaire's sudden collapse.

If this is true, can it therefore be said that when Yeats reverts to his original tragic purpose in the final version, the episodes appear to re-order themselves and point forward to the new ending? The new ending has at least the virtue of not implicating Guaire at all; he is now no longer required to act in a way which appears to be justified only by the dramatist's desire to solve his own problem as a narrator. But in order to describe in a more positive way the quality of the new version, we must look not at that structural feature—the chain of episodes—on which attention has so far been fixed, but consider also another element in the construction. This could be labelled 'the character of Seanchan', or, more accurately, the story of his death: 'the man that dies has the chief part in the story'.

Linking the various episodes, the beads on the string, there is the thread itself, the fasting Seanchan. He is the element in the play which was represented in *The Countess Cathleen* by the scenes between Aleel and Cathleen. In that play it was to some extent at odds with the original fable. In *The King's Threshold* it is co-terminous with the play itself, in one sense *is* all the play, or the 'chief part' in it, fully present from the beginning, not growing into it during the revision. And what the final revision did was simply to allow it to run its natural course to its predestined end. Yeats had his own set of metaphors for an element of this kind when he wrote in the Preface to *Poems 1899–1905*:

After I had learned to hold an audience for an act in prose I found that I had everything to learn over again in verse, for in dramatic prose one has to prepare principally for actions, and for the thoughts or emotions that bring them about or arise out of them; but in verse one has to do all this and to follow as well a more subtle sequence of cause and effect, that moves through vast sentiments and intricate thoughts that accompany action, but are not necessary to it. It is not very difficult to construct a fairly vigorous prose play, and then . . . to decorate it and encumber it with poetry. But a play of that kind will never move us poetically, because it does not uncover, as it were, that high, intellectual, delicately organized soul of men and of an action, that may not speak aloud if it do not speak in verse.[13]

Not all the terms and implications of this passage, in particular the contrast between verse and prose, are relevant. But the 'more subtle sequence', the intricate thoughts that accompany action and uncover its soul—these can be found in the play and do belong to its chief character.

II

The dying Seanchan, like the dying Samson, has been criticized for being too passive a protagonist. But he is rendered with a good deal of varied life. We hear about his family and his neighbours and his singing-school, so that his character acquires a solidity of specification matching the sense of place that was so lacking in *Sancan the Bard*. But the most vital element is Seanchan's struggle between vision and delirium. This is the inner story of his dying and has a progressive movement of its own, one that is cheated of its resolution in the earlier versions. It 'speaks aloud' in the imagery of his verse, which is destructive, joyful, 'apocalyptic', visionary— or mournful, diseased, delirious. The antithesis is established early in the play. The Oldest Pupil (called Senias in the first version) says, using a similitude that was to recur in Yeats's studies of the subjective man:

> for your hunger I could weep;
> And yet the hunger of the crane that starves
> Because the moonlight glittering on the pool
> And flinging a pale shadow has made it shy,
> Seems to me little more fantastical
> Than this that's blown into so great a trouble.[14]

Seanchan answers:

> There is much truth in that, for all things change
> At times, as if the moonlight altered them,
> And my mind alters as if it were the crane's;
> For when the heavy body has grown weak
> There's nothing that can tether the wild mind
> That being moonstruck and fantastical
> Goes where it fancies.

The Pupil's betrayal of his poetic faith is next associated by Seanchan with the changing moon. Later in the same episode with the Pupils comes the Nietzschean joy:

Have I not opened school on these bare steps,
And are not you the youngest of my scholars?
And I would have all know that when all falls
In ruin, poetry calls out in joy,
Being the scattering hand, the bursting pod,
The victim's joy among the holy flame,
God's laughter at the shattering of the world,
And now that joy laughs out and weeps and burns
On these bare steps.

This theme, too, of Dionysan art, has a long future history in Yeats's work, culminating in 'The Gyres' and 'Lapis Lazuli'.*

In the central portion of the play Seanchan is the Dionysan poet, and is therefore both benign and comminatory. The powers that oppose poetry, particularly the Mayor, the Monk, and the Soldier, are cursed as king's dogs, fools, and hypocrites, who require a tame song-bird for their god; but the girls who want to dance and make love are blessed in the speech beginning 'Yes, yes, go to the hurley'. This speech is placed close to one which shows the progressive movement towards weakness, delirium, and disease. Seanchan outrages beauty and charity by cursing the Princess and telling the story of the leper that blessed her mother:

> Hold out your hands,
> I will find out if they are contaminated . . .

and

> There are no sound hands among you. No sound hands.
> Away with you, away with all of you,
> You are all lepers. There is leprosy
> Among the plates and dishes that you have brought me.
> I would know why you have brought me leper's wine?
> [*He flings the wine in their faces.*

---

* Compare Nietzsche, *Birth of Tragedy*: 'We are to perceive how all that comes into being must be ready for a sorrowful end . . . We are really for brief moments Primordial Being itself, and feel its indomitable desire for being and joy in existence; the struggle, the pain, the destruction of phenomena, now appear to us as something necessary. We are pierced by the maddening sting of these pains at the very moment when we have become, as it were, one with the immeasurable primordial joy in existence, and when we anticipate, in Dionysan ecstasy, the indestructibility and eternity of this joy' (*Works*, tr. Levy, I. 128–9).

The moon-image recurs, infected. Seanchan's wavering mind sees everything as 'blessed' by its leprous hand:

> Where did I say the leprosy came from?
> I said it came out of a leper's hand
> And that he walked the highway; but that's folly,
> For he was walking up there in the sky
> And there he is even now with his white hand
> Thrust out of the blue air and blessing them
> With leprosy.
> *A Cripple.*   He's pointing at the moon
> That's coming out up yonder, and he calls it
> Leprous, because the daylight whitens it.

In the episode with Fedelm, Seanchan's images are again those of the joyful visionary, foreseeing the 'immeasurable primordial joy' of the future race:

> I lay awake,
> There had come a frenzy into the light of the stars
> And they were coming nearer and I knew
> All in a minute they were about to marry
> Clods out upon the plough-lands, to beget
> A mightier race than any that has been;

and

> The stars had come so near me that I caught
> Their singing; it was praise of that great race
> That would be haughty, mirthful, and white-bodied
> With a high head, and open hand, and how
> Laughing, it would take the mastery of the world.

The images of the infected moon, whose blessing is a curse, and the joyful, procreative stars, compose an antithesis mediating the 'more subtle sequence' that speaks aloud in verse. His ordeal, as it sharpens in intensity, has brought Seanchan to a vision of the contraries.

It is this issue and this way of stating it as what Seanchan, Chief Poet, sees, that fail to achieve resolution in the earlier versions. 'They breathe truth that breathe their words in pain.' [15] Seanchan's double vision becomes merely a pointless theatrical exercise in the psychopathology of hunger if it is not to be shown as expressing the truth about present and future worlds. The dead, infected world cannot so easily put itself to rights if it is, in this truth, a land of king's dogs and beauty poisoned at its source.

The earlier ending is wrong for a second and more positive reason. Seanchan's vision and his power to curse and prophesy are rooted in the gradual process of bodily derangement. This is depicted as of a kind which allows spiritual insight, images of good and evil, to become cruel and joyful and specific. Flesh is refined into knowledge. Where bodily weakness and mental vision are so intimately related, it is right that each should attain their natural goal, the grave which is also a watch-tower, the death that finishes the body but frees the spirit. But in the earlier versions we have to believe that bodily disorder ends in one way, with the recovery of life, and vision in another, with the acceptance of death—for it is essentially a vision of life through death, of the future race that supplants the one that is dying. Seanchan's gaze reaches beyond the dead world to the new life revealed to him by his suffering; but his story turns away, to Fedelm and Kinvara and the king's table again. 'The man that dies' to Guaire's world should die in the story, too, because the story is what he shares with Guaire and Guaire's well-meaning and high-principled allies, whom Seanchan in satire, prophecy and delirium has despoiled of fallacies. Only the Pupils, themselves finally ready for death, and the cripples, with their unfantastical hunger and superstitious awe of the poetic office, are cast out from Guaire's kingdom: all the story has gone to show that Guaire's place is with them, on the confines.

Yeats's last version of *The King's Threshold* is the best because it does not break the 'more subtle sequence', whereas in *The Countess Cathleen* it was the attempt to introduce such a sequence into a vigorous and self-consistent fable that caused some confusion to the design. *The King's Threshold*, although a much less ambitious piece, succeeds in being the kind of play that *The Countess Cathleen* failed to become through its long history of stitching and unstitching. Meanwhile, in *Deirdre*, Yeats tried his hand at constructing a play in which the episodes themselves have been transformed into the movements within 'the high, intellectual, delicately organized soul' of the chief character.

Chapter Three

Deirdre

I

ABOUT *Deirdre* the commentators disagree even more than usual. It is described as 'poetry written round the central crisis . . . not an expression of it'; 'a shadow-play, although sometimes the shadows perform an exquisite movement'.[1] It is 'pseudo-Elizabethan',[2] 'a charade', 'elegant and two-dimensional, the characters never come out at the audience'.[3] On the other side, we find that 'Yeats has travelled far from *The Land of Heart's Desire* and *Countess Cathleen*. There is no more remoteness from common experience, but, instead, an immediacy as terrible as that of Middleton, severest of Jacobean tragic poets.'[4] Deirdre's affirmation of love reflects a permanent reality of the human situation;[5] and Lennox Robinson testifies that 'Every part in the play is roundly written, every part has its variety, and of the one-act verse-plays it is the most supremely satisfactory.'[6]

Differing critical assumptions lead to these contrary conclusions, and it would not be hard to discover a Law of Parsimony which would permit one opinion or the other to be discarded. Taken in their variety, they do indicate the staginess (in both the bad and good senses) of *Deirdre*. A play which appears either austere or decorative, which admits or exiles reality, might stand as an emblem of the theatrical art, where at every point, in the author's brain as on the playhouse-stage, artificer and realist so habitually frustrate one another.

43

This staginess, in a narrower sense, enters into the first records of the play. The problem was, who was to perform the vast, central role, a virtuoso display-piece for an actress, on a scale that Yeats had not attempted before. Mrs. Patrick Campbell had her eye on it, but, according to Yeats, had had the wrong training in 'plays like *Mrs. Tanqueray*, where everything is done by a kind of magnificent hysteria';

This school reduces everything to an emotional least common denominator. It finds the scullion in the queen, because there are scullions in the audience but no queens. . . . A new school of acting is now growing up under the influence of the various attempts to create an intellectual drama, and of changes deeper than that. The new school seizes upon what is distinguished, solitary, proud even. One always got a little of this in Mrs. Emery when she was good, and one gets a great deal of it in Miss Darragh.[7]

It was not hysteria that Yeats sought in the creation and presentation of his central character, but energy: 'intensity of personal life, intonations that show . . . the strength, the essential moment of a man'.[8]

Of all Yeats's plays, *Deirdre* is the one where it is easiest—although still far from easy—to decipher some correspondence between play and the jumble of self-criticism, propaganda, and oracular sayings which constitute Yeats's reflections on the needs of the theatre at the time when *Deirdre* was being written and performed. *Energy* is a key-word, a masterful fullness of life, 'energy of soul'. It corresponds to or is transmuted into abundant personality; it is expressed (on the stage and in life) in the extravagant, personal, reckless gesture:

We, who are believers, cannot see reality anywhere but in the soul itself, and seeing it there we cannot do other than rejoice in every energy, whether of gesture, or of action, or of speech, coming out of the personality, the soul's image.[9]

This was a comparatively new complex of ideas. It was connected, as Thomas Parkinson has shown, with the poet's growing willingness to submit to the playwright's obligation to dramatize personalities, and with an increasing distaste for the unmoving and the silent, for the 'still life' and impersonality that had charac-

44

terized figure and landscape in the earlier poetry of 'essences and states of mind'.[10]

There were several different ways of justifying the concern with heroic and personal energies. There was the patriotic way:

an imaginative delight in energetic characters and extreme types, enlarges the energy of a people by the spectacle of energy.[11]

There was the psychological way:

The creative energy of men depends upon their believing that they have, within themselves, something immortal and imperishable, and that all else is but as an image in a looking-glass. So long as that belief is not a formal thing, a man will create out of a joyful energy, seeking little for any external test of an impulse that may be sacred, and looking for no foundation outside life itself.[12]

And there was the dramaturgical way. The stress on heroic energy supported the campaign against naturalism in the theatre and helped to shape its strategy. The 'more important' kind of drama, which is 'an activity of the souls of the characters' is 'an energy, an eddy of life, purified from everything but itself'.[13] Yeats's doctrine here shows an interesting affinity with the practice of Chapman or Dryden, who sought to fill their plays with heroic energies and to empty them of Shakespearian particularity, continually contriving exemplars of passionate virtue and Herculean strength and flame. For Yeats, Shakespeare appeared 'mixed with the whole spectacle of the world', but the characters in heroic drama live with an intensity that burns up their links with the world. It is this intensity, according to Yeats, that is the proper subject of drama:

If the subject of drama or any other art, were a man himself, an eddy of momentary breath, we might desire the contemplation of perfect characters; but the subject of all art is passion, and a passion can only be contemplated when separated by itself, purified of all but itself, and aroused into a perfect intensity by opposition with some other passion, or it may be with the law.[14]

It was the process of separation, purification, avoidance of distractions that counted when it came to establishing principles for the drama, and this process ran counter to the assumptions of the naturalistic drama as Yeats understood them. He argued, for example, that the dramatist must invent not the typical but the

45

exceptional personage. The 'typical' character as defined by the naturalistic school meant that a writer must create 'personifications of averages, of statistics, or even personified opinions, or men and women so faintly imagined that there is nothing about them to separate them from the crowd'.[15] But such characters are falsely fathered upon the poets by the propagandists. For the poets meant by the 'typical' character 'the character who must be typical of something which exists in all men because the writer has found it in his own mind'; they meant personages 'which startle us by being at once bizarre and an image of our own secret thoughts'.[16] 'A poet creates tragedy from his own soul, that soul which is alike in all men'[17]—the *anima mundi* itself. The exceptional, the heroic, the solitary, the Fool or the Queen, command response at the level where the poet's vision and experience as incarnate in his inventions speak to and awaken their simulacra in the spectator's heart. The spectator, like the magus Zoroaster, continually meets his own image, but walking upon the stage:

The greatest art symbolizes not those things that we have observed so much as those things that we have experienced, and when the imaginary saint or lover or hero moves us most deeply, it is the moment when he awakens within us for an instant our own heroism, our own sanctity, our own desire.[18]

It is the anti-naturalist who is most concerned with reality, because in this way he touches the 'intimate life' of the spectator, instead of presenting him, as the naturalist does, with personages in whom the inner life beats faintly because all their energy is taken up with the accurate imitation of life's surfaces. And the power of a theatre which acknowledges and encourages this deep and intimate communion of playwright and spectator is thaumaturgical indeed:

All creation requires one mind to make and one mind of enjoyment. The theatre can at rare moments create this one mind of enjoyment, and once created, it is like the mind of an individual in solitude, immeasurably bold—all is possible to it.[19]

Backed by arguments of this kind Yeats advocated a drama which bestowed primacy on speech. Speech is the only medium capable of developing the subtlety of expression needed to lay bare 'that which hides itself continually' in the depths of the soul.[20]

46

By the same token, the natural energy and subtle precision of this speech and the spectacle of the personage scrutinizing what is within him by the discipline of sincerity and logic will only be spoilt and diverted by the 'hysteria' that Yeats suspected in Mrs. Patrick Campbell, by elocutionary expertise or constantly varying attitudes:

When one requires the full attention of the mind, one must not weary it with any but the most needful changes of pitch and note, or by an irrelevant or obtrusive gesture.[21]

Let actors rehearse in barrels that they may be free to think of speech![22] Like Arthur Symons and Gordon Craig, Yeats stressed the theatrical value of immobility and silence. Scenery, too, full of possible distractions, must be austere and suggestive only. It must not compete with 'the illusion created by the actor, who belongs to a world with depth as well as height and breadth'.[23] The modern naturalist thinks continually about how his audience is going to behave, and is continually working to impress and manipulate it; instead of thinking about his own subject, he seeks 'external aids, remembered situations, tricks of the theatre',[24] but:

If we understand our own minds, and the things that are striving to utter themselves through our minds, we move others, not because we have understood or thought about those others, but because all life has the same root . . . the following of art is little different from the following of religion in the intense preoccupation that it demands. Somebody has said 'God asks nothing of the highest soul but attention'.[25]

An energy flowing from the depths of personality and expressed in a medium of subtlety, austerity, and restraint—this is what Yeats sought in the writing of *Deirdre* and expected the player of his principal part to understand. If it is true that the consolidation of the Abbey and its audience by 1906 allowed Yeats to be bolder than he had been before in aligning dramatic theory with dramatic practice, then *Deirdre* is, in some respects at least, recognizable as the kind of play that might have been expected to result from the conjunction. In *Deirdre* everything concentrates on the way the single heroic individual confronts her destiny. Our contemplation of this encounter is as little disturbed as possible by other elements, even by the presence, obligatory though it is, of

47

the other characters in her story. Unlike Synge, Yeats cuts the intrigue to the bone, subordinates Naoise very deliberately, and does the same with Conchubar.* They must not be permitted to diminish Deirdre's personal, heightened, exceptional existence. Yeats was striving to create a memorable character of the 'kind that follows us into our intimate life' because of the level at which it commands response, as do Odysseus, Don Quixote, or Hamlet, who are 'with us always'.[26] Yet, because the dramatist was obliged by his experience to acknowledge that certain kinds of artifice are unavoidable, this ideal had a year later to be discriminated more carefully. Homer and Cervantes were, after all, freer than Sophocles or Shakespeare, and their freedom was the measure of their greater access to energy and intimacy and personality:

I met an old man out fishing a year ago, who said to me, 'Don Quixote and Odysseus are always near to me'; and that is true for me also, for even Hamlet and Lear and Oedipus are more cloudy. No playwright ever has made or ever will make a character that will follow us out of the book as Don Quixote follows us out of the book, for no playwright can be wholly episodical, and when one constructs, bringing one's characters into complicated relations with one another, something impersonal comes into the story. Society, fate, 'tendency', something not quite human, begins to arrange the characters and to excite into action only so much of their humanity as they find it necessary to show one another.[27]

An irony of a more local but perhaps equally unavoidable kind attended the first performances of *Deirdre*. The choice of Miss Darragh rather than of Mrs. Campbell to play the part was another attempt to prevent depths and intimacy being disturbed more than could be helped by the glitter of artifice. But it seems to have had the contrary effect, according to W. G. Fay. Miss Darragh's sophisticated, professional style contrasted too much with the very different manner of the Abbey players: 'It

---

* Yeats would, I think, have been disappointed and surprised, even if unable to deny the connexion, at the way this play is related to *On Baile's Strand* and *The King's Threshold* by Parkinson (see below, p. 65), whom Ellmann follows: 'Deirdre and Naisi, Cuchulain, and Seanchan represent the reckless ideal and the kings with whom they war the inglorious reality (*Identity of Yeats* [London, 1954], p. 106).'

was like putting a Rolls-Royce to run a race with a lot of hill ponies.' *

II

Despite the frustrations that threatened it, the life of Deirdre herself, conceived—at any rate in some measure—as a practical expression of a complex of ideas about what the theatre ought to be and do, is the chief thing in the play, and dominates its design as neither Seanchan nor the Countess Cathleen dominate in their plays. The single episode which constitutes the plot is shaped to produce this effect, and everything the other characters do or say is intended to give us the measure of Deirdre and her situation.†

During the protasis, before the entry of Deirdre and Naoise, the audience is invited to ask, 'What kind of story is this?' This

---

* W. G. Fay and Catherine Carswell, *The Fays and the Abbey Theatre* (London, 1935), p. 208. Miss Darragh's appointment also offended the other players. Miss Darragh, whose real name was Letitia Marion Dallas, was later one of the founders of the Liverpool Repertory Theatre. She died in 1917. Mrs. Campbell eventually played *Deirdre* in Dublin and London in the last months of 1908. Yeats, who genuinely admired her art (see *Letters*, p. 360), began to compose what much later became *The Player Queen* with Mrs. Campbell in mind for the part of Decima.

† *Deirdre* was revised much less than *The Countess Cathleen* or *The King's Threshold*. The general effect of the revisions is to make Deirdre more prominent and central. (1) First version, 1907: in *Plays for an Irish Theatre*, Volume V., *The Poetical Works of William B. Yeats* (New York, 1907, Volume II), and, slightly revised, in *Collected Works* (Stratford-on-Avon, 1908, Volume II). (2) 'Alterations in "Deirdre",' November, 1908. Yeats wrote, in this four-page leaflet printed for insertion in *Plays for an Irish Theatre*, Volume V (see Wade, p. 79): 'There are two passages in the play which I always knew to be mere logic, mere bones, and yet, after many attempts, I thought it impossible to alter them. When, however, Mrs. Campbell offered to play the part, my imagination began to work again.' The two passages concern the first entrance of Deirdre and her later attempt to pretend to arouse Naoise's jealousy. The new version of the entrance had already been printed in the Appendix to Volume II of *Collected Works*. Both the new passages, with some further alterations, were incorporated in the text for the first time in *Deirdre*, 1911 (Wade, No. 86) and in *Plays for an Irish Theatre* (Stratford-on-Avon, 1911). (3) *Plays in Prose and Verse*, 1922. Yeats's note, dated 1922, is misleading: 'I have revised it a good deal of recent years, especially this last year.' The changes are not very considerable, but include one cut of about 25 lines. There are a few more small changes in the text in *Collected Plays* (1934). My quotations are from this edition.

element is stressed by the intentionally emphatic use which Yeats has made of the expository material forced upon him by his decision to plunge *in medias res,* and so is the feeling that there is somewhere hidden a pattern, or archetype, to which, if it can be found out, the story will be seen to conform. 'We are in a story,' says the First Musician in the opening lines, 'such a story as we sing':

> I have a story right, my wanderers,
> That has so mixed with fable in our songs
> That all seemed fabulous.

But the tale of Deirdre, Naoise, and Conchubar, which she now relates, in order to perfect its nature as a story asks for an ending, and then only will it win complete, professional approval:

> The tale were well enough
> Had it a finish.

Audience and tale-teller would then know what kind of story it is, whether happy or sad, and be able to judge it. They are about to be told:

> But gather close about that I may whisper
> The secrets of a king . . .
> I have been to Conchubar's house and followed up
> A crowd of servants going out and in . . .
> and came at length
> To a great room.

On this forboding note the Musician is interrupted by the entry of Fergus, who proceeds to offer his version of the story's end. It is to be reconciliation.

> *First Musician.* Are Deirdre and her lover tired of life?
> *Fergus.* You are not of this country or you'd know
> That they are in my charge and all forgiven.
> *First Musician.* We have no country but the roads of the world.

The 'roads of the world' tell them that 'an old man's love . . . is hard to cure', that 'old men are jealous': it is *that* kind of story, so their experience of stories tells them. They admit none of Fergus's attempts to qualify the pattern upon which the story seems to

them to be insisting, and they finally lead him back to the point
that had been reached just before his entrance:

There is a room in Conchubar's house, and there—

The sinister re-iteration of this note carries unimpeachable
authority for the audience, and makes Fergus's cheerful babble
convey the truth even while he denies it:

I know myself, and him, and your wild thought
Fed on extravagant poetry, and lit
By such a dazzle of old fabulous tales
That common things are lost, and all that's strange
Is true because 'twere pity if it were not.

This is another way of indicating that the professional storyteller recognizes an analogue when she sees one, and the next
moment Fergus's own tongue unwillingly stumbles across one
too when he urges the Musicians to begin an appropriate song for
the entrance of Deirdre and Naoise:

Begin, begin, of some old king and queen,
Of Lugaid Redstripe or another; no, not him,
He and his lady perished wretchedly.

The audience now knows that it is the Musicians rather than
Fergus who must be believed, and knows as well the kind of
story it is. The opening phase of the play is a device for subordinat-
ing interest in plot to interest in character. When Deirdre enters,
we know that her tale is about to end in tragedy, although we do
not know how she will confront this destiny, or when she herself
will learn the nature of the story she is in. In the next phase the
question is asked not by the spectator but by the *dramatis persona*
('What kind of story am I in?'), and, set against the key which the
spectator already holds to the answer, can be rephrased by him as
'What kind of person is this?'

From the moment of her entrance Deirdre is preparing herself
for the role that she considers appropriate to her story as she
understands it so far. Throughout the rest of the play there is a
similar bond between her choice of role and her diagnosis of
story. At this point, she puts on her jewellery and her paint:

These women have the raddle that they use
To make them brave and confident . . .
You'll help me, women.

51

She is ready to 'dress for the part', her share in the feast of forgive-ness. But the role she has chosen contravenes her instinctive feeling that the story which it is designed to fit is not the true story:

> My husband took these rubies from a king
> Of Surracha that was so murderous
> He seemed all glittering dragon. Now wearing them
> Myself wars on myself, for I myself—
> That do my husband's will, yet fear to do it—
> Grow dragonish to myself.*

Further omens—the chess-board of Lugaid, and the absence of a messenger from Conchubar to greet them—hint that the story is other than it seems. The fact that Fergus and Naoise refuse to attend to these hints, while Deirdre does, distinguishes her. Naoise reproaches her in words like those spoken by Fergus earlier: 'You have muddled yourself with old tales, seeing story-analogues where none exists':

> We must not speak or think as women do,
> That when the house is all a-bed sit up
> Marking among the ashes with a stick
> Till they are terrified.

But when Fergus and Naoise go out to see if any welcoming messenger is on his way, Deirdre turns to the Musicians with her question, 'What kind of story is this?' From them she gradually learns the true answer. They lay open to her the analogies that are crying out for recognition, and affirm that there are rules about the way people behave that will apply in her case as in any other. These they know about from their elder experience of love and 'the roads of the world'. But at first Deirdre misreads their hints and analogues:

> *First Musician.* I have heard he loved you
> As some old miser loves the dragon-stone
> He hides among the cobwebs near the roof.
> *Deirdre.* You mean that when a man who has loved like that
> Is after crossed, love drowns in its own flood,

---

* The episode of the jewellery was added in 1908 (*Plays for an Irish Theatre*, 1911, pp. 11–12) and makes Deirdre's entrance more full of lustre and decision than it is in the earlier version. See note on p. 49 above.

And that love drowned and floating is but hate;
And that a king who hates sleeps ill at night
Till he has killed; and that, though the day laughs,
We shall be dead at cock-crow.
First Musician.   You've not my thought.
When I lost one I loved distractedly,
I blamed my crafty rival and not him,
And fancied, till my passion had run out,
That could I carry him away with me,
And tell him all my love, I'd keep him yet.
Deirdre. Ah! now I catch your meaning, that this king
Will murder Naoise and keep me alive.

For Deirdre, this is much the worse of two bad stories. Proof that it is the one that is being told is given her when the Musician reveals to her the secret of the room in Conchubar's palace that she had twice tried to speak about before. It is a bridal chamber, adorned with magical stones that transform hate to love.

Deirdre's actions during the rest of the play can be summed up as a series of attempts to alter this story, as it were from inside the story itself. She can endeavour to control events only by influencing Naoise or Conchubar, and to this end she desperately plays one part after another in the hope of persuading them to change the story, or of persuading herself to endure it. The 'staginess' of the play is at its most incontrovertible in the character of its protagonist, who has to be a versatile 'actress'. The audience, using her breakdowns and failures to measure the effort that this costs her, is brought into the intimate life of the character by observing her struggle to disguise herself or to discover in herself a self that can outface the worst. We are continually reminded by Deirdre's own awareness of it that this is a tale in which the long-remembering harpers will find 'matter for their song'.[28]

Deirdre tries to persuade Naoise to escape by pretending that her jewels and adornments are intended to wake Conchubar's desire, but, when Fergus sees through her stratagem, she abandons this hastily assumed role of fickle woman and wants to destroy the beauty that has caused so much harm. Naoise tells her that they must conform to the story as it works out:

Leave the gods' handiwork unblotched, and wait
For their decision, our decision is past.

When the messenger from Conchubar finally reveals what is in his mind, Deirdre and Naoise plan a suitable end for their tale, an end different from the one designed by the king. They will behave like the characters in the old story of Lugaid Redstripe and his Queen:

> What do they say?
> That Lugaid Redstripe and that wife of his
> Sat at this chess-board, waiting for their end.
> They knew that there was nothing that could save them,
> And so played chess as they had any night
> For years, and waited for the stroke of sword.

And so they proceed to act out the analogue. But Deirdre, although she tries her best, finds that she cannot after all conform to her archetype:

> I cannot go on playing like that woman
> That had but the cold blood of the sea in her veins.

Passionate memories intervene between her and the due performance of the chosen role, which is abandoned before Conchubar makes his momentary appearance at the door to spy upon them. Naoise, twice mistaking the story, supposing first that Conchubar is honest and then that he is a coward, rushes out to fight him. Alone, Deirdre has thought the ending out again and begs the knife from the Musician, reminding her that the Musicians' part is to remember and record the tale:

> Women, if I die,
> If Naoise die this night, how will you praise?
> What words seek out? for that will stand to you;
> Being but dead we shall have many friends.
> All through your wanderings, the doors of kings
> Shall be thrown wider open, the poor man's hearth
> Heaped with new turf, because you are wearing this
> > [*Gives Musician a bracelet.*
> To show that you have Deirdre's story right.

But when Naoise is trapped, her pleas, undisguisedly desperate, are powerless to change the ends which each has chosen. Naoise is determined to die rather than to assent to Conchubar's bargain; Conchubar is resolved to have Deirdre, if needs be at the price of a life. When this has been exacted and Naoise is dead, Deirdre

immediately assumes her last role. This is her final means of controlling her fate and shaping it to the ends she desires. When she
adopts the semblance of a half-reluctant mistress, attracted by the
new lover yet preserving sufficient personal dignity to insist first
on paying her debt to the old one, assuring Conchubar that this
will make a good start to their new life together, and flaring up for
a moment into a wifely termagant admonishing him for the lack
of manliness he displays by his reluctance to grant her the favour,
she plays her most testing role. Its sustained complexity is the
measure of her determination, of the 'white-heat' at the heart of
it.* For all her previous disguisings had broken down; since
Naoise is dead, there are no analogues left, and no hopes either.
To finish the story in her way, and not Conchubar's, is her
sufficient inspiration. Her role here is in the same mode as her
other disguisings, but is a kind of imaginative triumph, because
distinguished by success as they were by failure.

III

The Countess Cathleen is a play essentially episodical. In *The King's
Threshold* the successive stage-pictures are threaded through by
the gradual exaltation of Seanchan towards his double vision. But
in *Deirdre* variety of episode and variety of stage-picture are both
subordinated to the central figure and her paradigm of roles. The
crises in the play are in Deirdre's personality: in the way she
comes to interpret her fate, and in the struggle to re-shape it by
playing a part. It is on this level that the audience is expected to
pay attention, and in this sense that the action of *Deirdre* may be
described as 'an activity of the soul of the character'. Whether it
is such an activity in a more specifically Yeatsian sense is another
question. Is the activity so purified that Deirdre seems to move to
the centre where 'all life has the same root' so that we see ourselves in her? The bond between the play and Yeats's notions of
drama appears, when it is further examined, to be of an extremely
paradoxical nature.

Yeats argued, in his theory of tragedy and tragic character, that

---

* 'Yeats used to say about Deirdre's performance—"Red-heat up to Naisi's
death, white-heat after he is dead"' (Lennox Robinson, in *Scattering Branches*,
p. 96).

character—the 'discrimination and definition of individuality' as Una Ellis-Fermor defined it in this connexion[29]—is 'continuously present in comedy alone'. In tragic art 'one distinguishes devices to exclude or lessen character'. 'Tragedy must always be a drowning and breaking of the dykes that separate man from man':

amid the great moments, when Timon orders his tomb, when Hamlet cries to Horatio 'absent thee from felicity awhile', when Antony names 'Of many thousand kisses the poor last,' all is lyricism, unmixed passion, 'the integrity of fire.' Nor does character ever attain to complete definition in these lamps ready for the taper.[30]

The definition of individuality, like assertive scenery and over-emphatic gestures, will ruin the spectator's trance-like absorption in those supreme moments, for the 'reverie' they induce—a state of sharing 'at the root of life' in the tragic personage's activity of soul—is exceedingly fragile:

Tragic art, passionate art, the drowner of dykes, the confounder of understanding, moves us by setting us to reverie, by alluring us almost to the intensity of trance. The persons upon the stage, let us say, greaten till they are humanity itself. We feel our minds expand convulsively or spread out slowly. . . . It was only by watching my own plays that I came to understand that this reverie, this twilight between sleep and waking, this bout of fencing, alike on the stage and in the mind, between man and phantom, this perilous path as on the edge of a sword, is the condition of tragic pleasure. If an actor becomes over emphatic . . . or even if an electric lamp that should have cast a reflected light from sky to sea, shows from behind the post of a door, I discover at once the proud fragility of dreams.[31]

In addition to his examples from Shakespeare, Yeats cited two other passages that induced the tragic reverie. One is the third Act of Synge's *Deirdre of the Sorrows*—'a reverie of passion that mounts and mounts till grief itself has carried [Deirdre] beyond grief into pure contemplation'.[32] The other is from his own *Deirdre*:

I am content with the players and myself, if I am moved for a while not by the contrasted sorrows of Deirdre and Naisi, but because the words have called up before me the image of a sea-born woman so distinctly that Deirdre seems by contrast to those unshaken eyelids that had but the sea's cold blood what I had wished her to seem, a wild bird in a cage.[33]

If my account of *Deirdre* is admissible, the question is not one of
deciding whether Yeats succeeded in writing a tragedy which
reached to the height of his theory, but whether the theory, or
this aspect of it, can usefully be applied to it at all. Although
Deirdre has her moments of beautiful, mindless desperation—a
wild bird in a cage—she is surely more full of character and artifice
than the theory admits. Her last phase, the phase of 'white-heat'
after the death of Naoise, is certainly not a phase of pure and
almost depersonalized grief, like that of Synge's heroine. With
controlled artifice, the staginess of the accomplished actress, she
presents to Conchubar a mask of deceit, which depends for its
success on its resourceful detail and on the verisimilitude with
which it appears to answer his wish while gaining her own end.
It is a battle of wit and will, resourceful wit balanced against the
old man's jealous will. Deirdre is not helpless in the grip of circumstance, as Lady Gregory had laid it down that the tragic
character ought to be,[34] but overcomes it by an act of the imagination, a role played out to the end. Her last, ambiguous words
assert her consciousness of triumph while holding out a false
promise to Conchubar. As for the spectator, trance or reverie
seems out of the question during the scene. 'We catch our breath,'
as Lennox Robinson remarked.

It was after he had written *Deirdre* that Yeats wrote:

The masks of tragedy contain neither character nor personal energy.
They are allied to decoration and to the abstract figures of Egyptian
temples. Before the mind can look out of their eyes the active will
perishes, hence their sorrowful calm. Joy is of the will which labours,
which overcomes obstacles, which knows triumph. The soul knows
its changes of state alone, and I think the motives of tragedy are not
related to action but to changes of state.[35]

The passage could be taken point by point as presenting the opposite of what is actually the case with *Deirdre*. The state of Deirdre's
soul—if by that is meant the deepest level of her personality, the
fundamental passion of her nature which motivates her behaviour
—changes not at all in the course of the play, but remains always
her passionate love for Naoise. Her active will never rests, but is
pitted turn by turn against her own weakness, against the Musicians, against Naoise; and finally against Conchubar; and the

'masks' which she adopts, her roles, are directly the instruments of this will, and gradually strengthen in both the definition of individuality and in the personal energy with which they are played out. She knows at last joyful triumph, which, according to Yeats, is the reward of comedy:

Comedy is joyous because all assumption of a part, of a personal mask, whether of the individualized face or of the grotesque face of farce, is a display of energy, and all energy is joyous.[36]

Here *energy* (and this might reasonably have remained unguessed from many of his other uses of the word) is the sign of comedy alone. In effect, *Deirdre* is nearer to what Yeats defined as comedy than to what he held tragedy to be. The irrelation between practice and theory has beome almost grotesque.

If Yeats suspected that his own version of the great tragic tale of the 'Irish Helen', the theme hallowed for him by the pen of the dying Synge, was queerly inapposite to his own thoughts about tragedy, he might well have been confused and disappointed by the difference between what he had done in the theatre and what he wanted to do. This was perhaps one cardinal reason, amongst many lesser ones, for the moratorium of ten years on play-writing. It is broken only by *The Green Helmet*, a comedy full of 'joyous energy' but a trifle none the less, and by the abortive attempt to start *The Player Queen*.* Apart from these, only the continuing process of revision of the plays already written, the endless concern with what he described, in the essay on 'The Tragic Theatre', as 'the wheels and pulleys necessary to the effect, but in themselves nothing', show that a second attempt, after so many at most precarious, and now faded, successes, was the recognition of a need.

* The date 1914 attached to *The Hour-Glass* in *Collected Plays* (1934) is misleading. The first prose-version of this play was first printed in 1903 (slightly revised in 1908 and 1911). A poetic version was being planned as early as June, 1903 (*Letters*, p. 393); the version in *Collected Plays*, partly in prose and partly in verse, was first printed in Gordon Craig's periodical *The Mask* in 1913 (Wade, No. 108, No. 110, No. 115).

PART TWO:
THE MYSTERY
TO COME

I wanted a theatre where the greatest passions and all
the permanent interests of men might be displayed
that we might find them not alone over a book but,
as I said again and again, lover by lover, friend by
friend. All I wanted was impossible, and I wore out
my youth in its pursuit, but now I know it is the
mystery to come.

—Pages from a Diary
Written in Nineteen Hundred and Thirty

Chapter Four

The Cuchulain Plays

Even though he represent no man of worth in his art, the worth
of his own mind becomes the inheritance of his people.

I

IN one of the papers from *Samhain* (1905) in 'The Irish
Dramatic Movement' Yeats writes of his rejection of the
'white phantoms' of the falsely idealized dramatic character, and criticizes *Caste* as an example of the conventional
idealism of the English theatre:

the central persons, the man and woman that created the dramatic
excitement, such as it was, had not characters of any kind, being vague
ideals, perfection as it is imagined by a commonplace mind. The
audience could give them its sympathy without the labour that comes
from awakening knowledge. If the dramatist had put into his play
whatever man or woman of his acquaintance seemed to come closest
to perfection, he would have had to make it a study, among other
things, of the little petty faults and perverted desires that arise out of
the nature or its surroundings. He would have troubled that admiring
audience by making a self-indulgent sympathy more difficult.[1]

When Yeats chose the life and death of Cuchulain as the subject
of five plays (which he came to think of as a coherent series), this
'antiquated romantic stuff', as the Old Man calls it in *The Death
of Cuchulain*,[2] did not tempt him to romantic idealization of
character and theme. He laboured to awaken knowledge in his
audience by giving them the oblique view and engendering his

conflicts from a continuous interplay of ironic meanings. It was not simply that Yeats had a sceptical or reserved attitude towards the antique story. His point of view entails a generous recognition of the value of heroic revolt, courage, and love; but they are placed in a context which proves tragic because of some element which is thwarting and contradictory in the nature of the heroic acts, the man who performs them, the spirit which inspires them, or the world in which they are done. This element does not take the form of a commentary, something outside the business of the plays; it is a part of their construction, and helps to create the tensions which make them dramatic.

The first of these plays is *On Baile's Strand*. The version of 1903 differs a good deal from the version of 1906.* The source is the story called 'The Only Son of Aoife' in Lady Gregory's *Cuchulain of Muirthemne*.[3] This relates how Conlaoch, the son of Aoife and Cuchulain, had been brought up by his mother in ignorance of his father's identity because of the jealous loathing she had conceived for Cuchulain, who defeated her in battle, became her lover, and then, unaware that she had borne a son, abandoned her for marriage to Emer. Conlaoch, now grown to manhood, arrives at Baile's Strand where the High King Conchubar is holding court with his counsellors and warriors. Aoife has caused her son to take an oath to challenge the greatest champion of Ireland without revealing whose son he is. Cuchulain accepts the challenge, but learns too late, when the boy is mortally wounded, whom he has killed. Madness descends upon the hero and he fights the sea.

Of all the Abbey plays, *On Baile's Strand*, which has been called one of 'the best poetic plays of this century'[4] and which generated several spurts of creative excitement in Yeats himself,[5] seems most at home with the material of the elder world in which it is set. In it, as well as in *The Green Helmet*, we can most clearly trace what it was that Lady Gregory's two volumes of paraphrased legend contributed to the dramatist's imagination. Lady Gregory's work enabled him to see the legendary world as a whole, to hold it in

* The 1903 version was printed in *In the Seven Woods* (Cuala Press, Dublin, 1903) and Volume III of *Plays for an Irish Theatre* (1904); the revised version first appeared in *Poems 1899–1905* (London and Dublin, 1906). My quotations are from this text except where otherwise stated.

the hollow of his imagination, and to vitalize it with habits, customs, and manners. The trappings of Cuchulain in *On Baile's Strand*, the witches, warriors, hunt, and camp, and the allusions with which the speakers amplify passion and argument, are remotely clear and strange because they derive from a single vision of a past world; they are not distant from us because they are muzzy or arbitrary but because they are defined. The outlines of the story itself Yeats could and did get from elsewhere. Although Yeats made the story which I have just summarized from *Cuchulain of Muirthemne* into the climax of his play, even in the first version he added many invented incidents. There is, first, the framing underplot of the Blind Man and the Fool. They are not only expositors, but are needed for the most theatrically effective moment in the play, which several commentators have praised,[6] the moment of agony when Cuchulain learns whom he has killed. It has also been remarked that their roles parody and change places with those of Cuchulain and Conchubar:

> the blind man
> Has need of the fool's eyesight and strong body,
> While the poor fool has need of the other's wit,
> And night and day is up to his ears in mischief
> That the blind man imagines.[7]

This too is how warrior and ruler serve each other. Yeats brings the relationship to life first by stressing the differences between Cuchulain's band of young and yeasty fighters and Conchubar's group of grave, ancient counsellors. He is also departing from his source in a point vital to his reading of the story when his Cuchulain accepts Conlaoch's challenge not unhesitatingly (as he does in the source) but because he is commanded to do so by the King, and because his understanding has been corrupted by the persuasion that his strange fondness for the young man has been engendered by witchcraft.

This new material, bearing on the relation between king and hero, is faintly handled in the first version, but very greatly expanded in the second version. Yeats substitutes for the discussion of Conchubar's plan for building his city (in the first version) a prolonged debate between the two men (in the second). It culminates in a ceremony at which Cuchulain swears an oath of obedience to Conchubar and his heirs. Not until this has been done does the story, in Lady Gregory's sense, begin.

Such an arrangement of the tale, with so much emphasis on preliminaries (for Conlaoch does not enter until a good half of the play is done), might have had a strangely muffling and delaying effect upon the culminating, brutal irony of the father's fight with the son. But Yeats uses his plot, made up of two episodes instead of one, to tangle and thicken the ironies and to organize within and around his hero the perturbations proper to a protagonist of stature. We share in Cuchulain's 'intimate life' and 'activity of soul'.

Cuchulain has been troubling the kingdom. Without children himself, he will not acknowledge those of his master. The quarrel is designed to bring out the contrast between the hero's turbulence and the ruler's responsibilities. For the play, in both its versions, is about how the building of a city and a kingdom destroys another kind of life. The High King complains that:

> every day my children come and say
> 'This man is growing harder to endure.
> How can we be at safety with this man,
> That nobody can buy or bid or bind?
> We shall be at his mercy when you are gone.
> He burns the earth as if it were a fire,
> And time can never touch him.'

' I do not like your children', says Cuchulain:

> They have no pith,
> No marrow in their bones, and will lie soft
> Where you and I lie hard.

Conchubar's heirs seem ghostly and insignificant to the hero, who is unbiddable because he has no son to care for and constrain him. Instead, he has only a fantastic and overweening notion of what a child of his might be—a man that would face 'Even myself in battle'. 'Now as ever', declares Conchubar,

> You mock at every measurable hope,
> And would have nothing or impossible things.
> What eye has ever looked upon the child
> Would satisfy a mind like that!

But although Cuchulain dreams of a new generation able to challenge the splendour of his own, the dream itself only compensates for the sense of present wanting:

> I know you to the bone.
> I have heard you cry—aye, in your very sleep—
> 'I have no son!' and with such bitterness
> That I have gone upon my knees and prayed
> That it might be amended.

This ominous play upon the theme of fatherhood deepens the narrative. The debate is linked in other ways with the coming of Conlaoch. His finding the shore insufficiently guarded has brought the issue of Cuchulain's irresponsibility to a head; and the dramatic excitement is greater because Conlaoch's entrance follows immediately upon the taking of the oath, whereas in the first version his arrival merely interrupts the mild, though not inconsequential, discussion of Conchubar's plan to rebuild his capital city. Parkinson has also drawn attention to the wider field of reference, from this play to other plays, of which the completer design of the second version makes us aware:

the major subject of Yeats' Abbey dramas was the conflict between the fixed palpable world of human affairs (Guaire, Conchubar) and the world of passion and aspiration, which is beyond reason, system, or office (Seanchan, Cuchulain). The basic split in the plays is that between the institutional world—limited, tame, calculating, interested in the virtue of fixed character—and the personal world—exuberant, carefree, wild, affirming the values of intense personality.[8]

But the greatest interest of the new episode is the way in which it affects our view of Cuchulain's tragedy in the second half of the play. Variations on the subjects that are talked about during the debate and oath-taking are played through during the meeting with Conlaoch, where the attitudes of king and hero are put to the test of Conlaoch and emerge passionately disordered and ironically interchangeable. This is because the links that have been mentioned are more than merely narrative connexions. They are often vital antitheses, and hence lead to the lively interaction of the two episodes.

When even his own troopers wish Cuchulain to take the oath and become 'as biddable as a house-dog', he submits:

> You've wives and children now,
> And for that reason cannot follow one
> That lives like a bird's flight from tree to tree.

He agrees to offer up his uncaged existence through a protective ritual which is designed to ward off the temptations of the shape-changers as they are practised upon the nameless and houseless man. From henceforth his sword will, in the words of the oath,

> have for master none
> But the threshold and hearthstone.

The stability seemingly achieved through this submission next breaks down into the tragedy in which the hero is destroyed. Conchubar's paramount authority, strengthened by the oath, is once more the agent responsible.

When the Young Man from Aoife's country arrives, Conchubar commands Cuchulain to accept the challenge, while Cuchulain, touched by his half-familiar beauty, seeks peace and order in Conlaoch's friendship.[9] For the second time in the play the king requires the hero to thwart his 'energy of soul' by obeying him. Cuchulain is seen complete when he is seen trapped in this dilemma. It is created by the blindness of authority to whatever force it is that keeps the heroic spindle whirling round. But, on this second occasion, the issue has shifted, as the armed stranger begins to take on the aspect of a son. When Conchubar orders Cuchulain to fight the Young Man who will not tell his name, he is demanding the subversion in Cuchulain of that calm life of the threshold and the hearthstone, the instinctive yearning for naming instead of namelessness, which the king himself had earlier in the play bound him with, first by his reproaches and then by the oath. The authority of the Blind Man, which appears consistent in its continual demand for obedience, really asks that Cuchulain strain both ways, from turbulence into peace, and then, when that is being achieved, into houseless turbulence once more.

Thus Yeats makes a double knot out of his singly knotted source. The two central episodes are interlocked by means of certain thematic links, so that the second episode draws meaning from the first. These links serve not only to make the tale more exciting; they also tighten by twisting, making the inward life of Cuchulain tenser by pulling it in different directions. Thus to Conchubar in the first episode the childlessness and faithlessness of the hero had been the reasons for his turbulence and a cause for pride with Cuchulain himself:

> I'll not be bound.
> I'll dance or hunt, or quarrel or make love,
> Wherever and whenever I've a mind to.

In the second episode Cuchulain instinctively reaches towards alliance and fatherhood; it seems that the fantastic and impossible wish for a son that will match up to Cuchulain's dream of a son— which in the first episode was an index of his heroic excess—is about to be realized:

> Boy, I would meet them all in arms
> If I'd a son like you. He would avenge me . . .
> But I'd need no avenger. You and I
> Would scatter them like water from a dish.

Conlaoch is the man whom Conchubar believed could not exist and now cannot discern, although Cuchulain is just beginning to see him.

There is, too, the theme of Queen Aoife, whose love turned to hatred. When, during the debate, Cuchulain had argued for heroic wildness he had justified his contempt for ordinary women and his rejection of all that is settled in love by recalling the fierce beauties of Aoife.[10] When Conchubar had reminded him that Aoife now hated him, he had answered by defining heroical love as the paradoxical conjunction of love and hate:

> I never have known love but as a kiss
> In the mid-battle, and a difficult truce
> Of oil and water, candles and dark night,
> Hillside and hollow, the hot-footed sun,
> And the cold sliding, slippery-footed moon—
> A brief forgiveness between opposites
> That have been hatreds for three times the age
> Of this long-'stablished ground.

This heroical love that denies the threshold and the hearthstone

67

had been repudiated in the oath's chant against the witches, who

> will give him kiss for kiss
> While they murmur, 'After this
> Hatred may be sweet to the taste';
> Those wild hands that have embraced
> All his body can but shove
> At the burning wheel of love
> Till the side of hate comes up.

And when Aoife's son faces him, the likeness to his mother wakens in Cuchulain a love which seeks not a brief forgiveness but a life of friendly play. Not opposite meets opposite, but likeness likeness. The likeness is charged with irony: these are two sons whose fathers would, or could, kill them:

> Boy,
> If I had fought my father, he'd have killed me
> As certainly as if I had a son,
> And fought with him I should be deadly to him.

It is Conchubar's endeavour to stir up the dreadful implications of a likeness such as that. By reminding Cuchulain that Conlaoch is the emissary of Aoife he seeks to bring about that transformation of love into hatred which Cuchulain in his turbulence had acknowledged and affirmed, but which the oath had repudiated. Thus Conchubar seeks to bring back the tumult which he had earlier tried to allay and so unknowingly subjects them all to Aoife's evil will. The tragic authority, since it wants his sword in battle, wishes Cuchulain to re-assume the heroic antinomies which the hero, at the ruler's own behest, had shed.

These opposites are finely organized in the act of Cuchulain's striking the High King. It is the moment of almost wordless action when the antinomies blaze forth.

During the course of the second episode the play has taken another turn. The warriors, backed by Conchubar, challenge Conlaoch, and Cuchulain moves into his old place, fronting and defying the ruler, not on behalf of the heroic freedom, but for the new love. But he is appalled at his own deed when he strikes at the High King in the passion of revolt. Formerly, even the defence of his own freedom had concluded in submission, and it is right that the Cuchulain who took the oath should now see the

68

blow at Conchubar as the corruption of his own nature by witch-craft having its source in the Young Man who has bewitched him into friendship. Conchubar has now got the Cuchulain he wanted: the oath-taker who respects his sacred authority and goes out to fight his enemy. The irony is that this Cuchulain is also the one who, in the act of doing so, rejects and regards as corrupted the 'energy of soul', aroused by Conlaoch's significant likeness, which moves him towards peace and fatherhood and towards the threshold and the hearthstone—those very things which had been the substance and rationale of the oath that Conchubar had made him take. It is Aoife's will, the 'will of woman at her wildest',[11] that is now being fulfilled. In the hero, both the old heroic and the new anti-heroic unities of being have been manipulated to destroy each other. Confusion has fallen upon his thought.

The father who kills his son butchers his own image. Yeats has transformed this simple horror into a tangled drama of self-destruction by using his two episodes to 'arrange much complicated life into a single action'.[12] Fate and Conchubar combine to transform heroic energy into madness, and the Fool and the Blind Man are left as the masters of the scene.

II

In *The Golden Helmet*, re-written as *The Green Helmet* (1908 and 1910), Yeats has again worked by juxtaposing two episodes: the quarrel of the chieftains, and the test for the championship of Ulster. As Birgit Bjersby has pointed out, Yeats has put the episodes together into a single action by departing from his sources and combining Bricriu, the maker of discord, and CuRoi, the tester, into the single figure of the Red Man.[13] The knot woven from the two subjects is untied with a single movement when Cuchulain offers his head to the Red Man. So he pays the debt imposed by the Red Man as his condition for the ending of the strife, and gains the championship not as 'the strongest' (the claim that has led to irresolvable strife amongst the warriors) but as the one who is 'without fear',[14] the gay hero, proper to the 'gay animated stage not too far from the mood of the world' which Yeats wanted in the play.[15] Thus the play concludes with a comic irony: the champion turns out not to be the mightiest but the most comely-hearted, the one who had earlier attempted to resolve discord into harmony by turning the coveted prize, the golden helmet, into a drinking-cup to be shared by all; and it is he who is greeted by the Red Man as one who 'shall win many battles with laughing lips and endure wounding and betrayal without bitterness of heart'.[16] In this Cuchulain there is no tragic dichotomy between what he is and what he is made to do.

But the tragedy of heroic circumstance is revived once more in the third of the Cuchulain plays, *At the Hawk's Well* (finished in 1916). It is about the courage without which there can be no heroic desire, but which is made the means to thwart it. The Old Man has been waiting by the well for fifty years for a chance to drink the mysteriously flowing water, but each time the water has bubbled out he has been cheated of it by the 'deceivers', the dancers who guard the well in the form of hawks. Into their 'unfaltering, unmoistened eyes' he dares not look; although he has the desire, he lacks the courage, and whenever the water gushes their dance lulls him into a strengthless sleep. Cuchulain enters and learns this story. Then the silent Guardian of the Well becomes possessed by the hawk, the terrible life of the deity slides through her veins and reveals itself to Cuchulain in the gaze of the hawk's eyes. He stares into them, and so becomes subjected to the curse predicted by the Old Man:

> There falls a curse
> On all who have gazed in her unmoistened eyes . . .
> That curse may be
> Never to win a woman's love and keep it;
> Or always to mix hatred in the love;
> Or it may be that she will kill your children,
> That you will find them, their throats torn and bloody,
> Or that you will be so maddened that you kill them
> With your own hand.[17]

Then Cuchulain is lured from the flowing water by her dance, and at the same moment the Old Man, who has covered his head from the hawk's gaze, falls into his helpless sleep. The hero comes back to find that the well is dry again, and to learn that the warrior-women of the hills are roused against him. Shouldering his spear, he leaves the sacred mountain to confront with courage the bitter life of war.

70

The symbolic referents of the water and the hawk have been worked out by many commentators, but their general meaning in the play is plain, and sufficiently full to subserve the purposes of dramatic action. The water represents wisdom or immortality (either or both) or love unmixed with hatred (but surely not, as T. R. Henn seems to suggest, sexual virility).[18] But it is truer to what is in the play to see it as simply the one precious and mysterious gift that will release Cuchulain and the Old Man, the one from the toils of old age and the other from the bitter entanglements of the heroic fate, from the divided and thwarted life of the hero of *On Baile's Strand*. The guardian hawk that lulls and lures is deceit and illusion that destroy Cuchulain's unity of being, or confound his search for it. She is the 'inhuman, bitter glory', 'the persecution of the abstract'. She resembles Fand the Woman of the Sidhe in *The Only Jealousy of Emer* and Aoife in *The Death of Cuchulain*,[19] with whom in *At the Hawk's Well* she is in some sort of league (but not, I think, in this play to be identified with her, as Birgit Bjersby and Donald R. Pearce suppose).[20]

The courage of the hero is the theme which ties together the play's two episodes. They function in the design like protasis and catastrophe. It is courage which manifests itself as the major antinomy in the moment when fate is rendered through dramatic action—Cuchulain's behaviour as the hawk reveals itself and dances. The protasis is, as it was in *On Baile's Strand*, more than a mere exposition, but Yeats uses it with much greater economy and effect than he had in the earlier Cuchulain plays. The timidity and withered condition of the Old Man, the expositor, result from his long years of failure to face the demon. He is all, in respect of courage, that Cuchulain is not:

YOUNG MAN

My luck is strong,
It will not leave me waiting, nor will they
That dance among the stones put me asleep;
If I grow drowsy I can pierce my foot.

OLD MAN

No, do not pierce it, for the foot is tender,
It feels pain much.

71

The Old Man has never dared to gaze into the hawk's eyes; he has not risked the curse, and now is cursed with vain senescence. Dramatically, he is Cuchulain's foil.

This preparation gives full weight of meaning to the moment when the hawk manifests itself. As the Old Man hides from the terrifying eyes, heroic courage gazes into them. Ironically, his act betrays Cuchulain. His courage robs him of what the courage was for—its prize, the sacred water; it commits him to the curse, and to the dance which leads him away from undivided being. We can understand why Yeats wrote of spitting upon the dancers painted by Degas,[21] when we see this dancer 'moving like a hawk'; she must both attract and destroy; she mimics the bird whose cruelty is inseparable from its beauty and herself has something of 'the supreme beauty which is accursed'.[22] What makes *At the Hawk's Well* a play and not a symbolist poem is the way in which the contradictory nature of heroic courage is prepared for and acted out through the deed and character of the hero. Cuchulain's movement of courage expresses his nature, but it also transforms him into a victim. What he is betrays him in its acting-out.

At the same time the other character, the Old Man, makes it plain that for Cuchulain to be less than himself is no escape either. To gaze into the hawk's eyes earns Cuchulain only the curse of self-division, the unhoused condition, the mixing of hatred and impermanence with love. But the failure to dare gets no reward either, only withering and self-despite. The curse is on Cuchulain's betraying courage; it now wears the colours of doom and of the death of Conlaoch. But the play ends, as do *Deirdre* and *The Herne's Egg*, in an assertion of identity and of the heroic Name, as Cuchulain leaves the stage shouldering his spear:

> He comes! Cuchulain, son of Sualtam, comes![23]

III

The Only Jealousy of Emer is perhaps the most intricately plotted of the Yeatsian Noh plays.* Despite its relatively complicated

---

* There are three versions. The first was finished in 1918, the second is a rewriting in prose, *Fighting the Waves* (written in 1928 and printed in *Wheels*

story, the ironic meanings are at their clearest, as though practice was bringing Yeats nearer to perfection. They attend upon the theme of love.

Cuchulain, after fighting the sea, lies in death watched over by his wife Emer and his mistress Eithne Inguba. When the body wakens to life at Eithne's kiss, it is seen to be possessed by the god Bricriu, the maker of discord. He offers to restore the hero's life on condition that Emer renounces her hope that Cuchulain's love will return at long last to her. He shows her the Ghost of Cuchulain being tempted by Fand, the Woman of the Sidhe, Bricriu's enemy; she is drawing the Ghost away to a life of immortal and inhuman love, and is resisted only by the Ghost's memories of Emer's earthly love. The Ghost is upon the point of yielding when Emer saves him by her renunciation, passionately withheld until this moment. But Cuchulain's first words as he wakes to life are a cry for Eithne Inguba.

The final episode is differently managed in the first and in the last versions. In the first, the renunciation breaks into the colloquy between the Ghost and Fand, and is followed by speeches from the Ghost which show his final realization of the folly of a deathless love which cannot experience suffering or memory:

> How could you know
> That man is held to those whom he has loved
> By pain they gave, or pain that he has given,
> Intricacies of pain.[24]

Fand rejects him as a man 'knotted in impurity', and there follows

---

and Butterflies, 1934), and the third is the version in Collected Plays. I use the last version, but refer also to the first as it is found in Four Plays for Dancers (1921). Yeats first heard about the Japanese Noh plays from Ezra Pound in the winter of 1913–14 (see the essay 'Swedenborg, Mediums, and the Desolate Places' in Lady Gregory's Visions and Beliefs, II. 333). At the Hawk's Well, The Only Jealousy of Emer, The Dreaming of the Bones, Calvary, and The Death of Cuchulain are the plays which most clearly show deliberate imitation of Noh techniques in their use of a 'unifying image', a dance, masks, and a chorus detached from the action. To a lesser degree the influence of the Noh can be detected in Purgatory and even in the prose-plays The Resurrection and The Words upon the Window-pane. For a useful study, see Earl Miner's The Japanese Tradition in British and American Literature (Princeton, 1958), pp. 251–65.

a quarrel between Fand and Bricriu. The last version omits all this, and places Emer's renunciation almost at the end of the play when Fand and the Ghost are just about to take horse for the Country-under-Wave. By these changes Yeats has greatly tightened the dramatic rhythm, but at the cost of making the themes slightly less clear and the interpenetration of natural and supernatural less intimate.

The major irony of the play is clear enough, though, especially when it is read in the light of the gradually sharpening ironies of the previous Cuchulain plays. Emer's renunciation of Cuchulain's love is her greatest act of love towards him. This is the same technique for the climactic moment of action as had been used in *At the Hawk's Well*. The loving wife must act so, for that is the ground of her being, but the act itself cancels out all hope of fulfilment for the loving nature from which it sprang, just as the hero's courage put out of reach for ever the prize which courage was designed to win. Her deed is solitary, 'self-delighting and self-affrighting', and by definition cannot be known to or recognized by the man whom Emer saves. A passage in the Preface to *Fighting the Waves* is relevant:

Here in Ireland we have come to think of self-sacrifice, when worthy of public honour, as the act of some man at the moment when he is least himself, most completely the crowd. The heroic act, as it descends through tradition, is an act done because a man is himself, because, being himself, he can ask nothing of other men but room amid remembered tragedies; a sacrifice of himself to himself, almost, so little may he bargain, of the moment to the moment.[25]

Emer's heroic deed, like Cuchulain's in *At the Hawk's Well*, is an assertion of her identity, of her name as loving wife, and her only reward, like Deirdre's, is that the long-remembering harpers shall have matter for their song.

But Emer here has a dimension which is absent from the Cuchulain of *At the Hawk's Well*. Her act is of such a character that it knows its consequence, and this is necessitated by the conditions under which it is performed. She does not find, after she has asserted her nature, that her destiny is in consequence to suffer its frustration; she chooses this destiny. She does not, as Cuchulain in the previous play does, dare the curse as part of the adventure,

74

but chooses to be cursed. For she is fulfilling her side of the bargain with Bricriu and knows what is bound to follow:

> He'll never sit beside you at the hearth
> Or make old bones, but die of wounds and toil
> On some far shore or mountain, a strange woman
> Beside his mattress.[26]

Her assent to the bargain is deliberate, and the nature of the bargain, as not in *The Golden Helmet*, is that neither side is pretending, so that the bargain cannot be comically evaded. Nothing Emer does is founded on a mistaking. She is more the heroine of the moral choice than any of Yeats's earlier protagonists, much more so than the Countess Cathleen, who, as we have seen, was never really given a chance to 'choose', and whose bargain is eventually annulled by heavenly justice. The difference shows Yeats's progression in the bleaker ironies.

Much more could, and has, been said about *The Only Jealousy*, in particular about 'those little known convictions about the nature and history of a woman's beauty', which Robartes found in the *Speculum* of Gyraldus and with which Yeats declared that he had filled the play.[27] But, although they are in the play, it is not, properly speaking, about them, but about the acting-out of Emer's dilemma. It was possible for W. Y. Tindall to claim that at first sight he found Emer's action unintelligible,[28] but the interpretation which he finally offers us ('man's victory over flux' and Fand as the Machine) almost suggests that he was not looking for a drama at all but for an enemy code which he could break. And Birgit Bjersby, who was interested in the correspondences between the play and the philosophical mythology, gives an account of them that seems to ignore all that makes *The Only Jealousy* an intelligible theatrical structure.[29] Yeats, although he enjoyed bringing into the play numerous echoes of the System, had not much desire that they should seriously distract the audience from the business of his stage. The descriptions of Woman's or Fand's beauty in the terminology of the phases of the moon, which we find in the Musicians' songs, help to create the chill, lofty, and allusive tone, which is a thing in itself, carried alive into the heart without need for glossing. The songs are, furthermore, detached from the play, in accordance with the principles of the Noh drama as Yeats understood them. They are a frame for the tragic struggle; they modulate towards it and away from it, but they do not enter into it. The notion of the Ghost lingering by its abode is a commonplace of tradition, and Yeats does not attempt to bestow upon it more than a hint of the elaborate schematizations that he was working out for the 'Soul in Judgement' sections of *A Vision*. The allusions to the phases of the moon in Fand's speeches work similarly to those in the musicians' songs. They sound the note of a remote, ordered, and inhuman world proper to the speech of a supernatural personage; to track them down to their lair in 'Gyraldus' and elsewhere does not seem to shed a great deal of light on the function in the drama of the character who speaks them.

What does need placing more firmly in an account of the play itself is the whole episode of Fand and the Ghost. As a dramatic device it does, I should guess, three things. It actualizes more vividly than anything merely related could have done the interpenetration of natural and supernatural which is the world of the play. It builds up tension as Emer watches it (like some dreadful sight seen in Friar Bacon's prospective glass); she resists up to and beyond the moment when the Ghost yields, and by this means the untying of the knot by her renunciation is delayed enough to point the desperate pain of her decision, and sudden and climactic enough to dismiss the demons from the play and break the interlocking of natural and supernatural worlds. Lastly, in depicting the character of the Ghost's resistance, it strengthens the ironies in the theme of love, because that resistance is compounded of his memories of Emer as bride and wife, whom when he was alive he deserted and when he is restored to life he puts by.

Yet a difficulty remains, a difficulty about the kind of temptation that Fand offers and represents. It is true that an assumption of the play must be that it is better to have Cuchulain alive than dead, whatever death may be, and that Fand, as the creature from the sea that has drowned Cuchulain, is substantially just Death itself. But Fand's characterization as a temptress cuts across her role as 'that which is not life', and what she offers is an immortal, if inhuman, love, where 'nothing but beauty can remain'. This Oisin-like state seems appropriate enough as the fate after death of the mythological hero. The feeling muddles our view of Emer's condition: from what, after all, is she saving him? It even suggests that Yeats's desire to put some of his 'little-known convictions' into his latest portrait of a Woman of the Sidhe, to plant in Ireland what he plucked in Byzantium, may have disordered his sense of the theatre—that Fand is what she is and offers what she does offer because Michael Robartes grasped at the pen. It might have been better if the Ghost's condition had been represented more neutrally, as a drawing away into some underworld of strengthless shades. It is probably significant that, when he re-wrote the play in prose 'to free it from abstraction and con-fusion',[30] Yeats reduced or evaded the problem by cutting out all the words set down for Fand and the Ghost and leaving her only her dance.

IV

The Death of Cuchulain is based upon the version of the story con-tained in the last two chapters of Lady Gregory's *Cuchulain of Muirthemne*. It makes special use of three key-incidents in it: the war-goddess's device of a treacherous message, delivered by Cuchulain's mistress, to the beleaguered hero; the death itself against the 'pillar-stone west of the lake' on the plain of Muir-themne; and the lamentation of Emer who 'took the head of Cuchulain in her hands, and she washed it clean, and put a silk cloth about it, and she held it to her breast; and she began to cry heavily over it'.[31]

Yeats wrote to Ethel Mannin in October, 1938:

Goethe said that the poet needs all philosophy but must keep it out of his work. I am writing a play on the death of Cuchulain, an episode or two from the old epic. My 'private philosophy' is there but there must be no sign of it; all must be like an old faery tale. It guided me to certain conclusions but I do not write it.[32]

I would draw a different inference from this passage than does F. A. C. Wilson who in his *W. B. Yeats and Tradition* has written at greater length on this play than any other scholar. It clearly affirms the continuing primacy, so far as the Cuchulain plays are concerned, of a theatrical rather than a symbolist strategy. Yeats still desires to 'show events' and still needs that roomful of people sharing one lofty emotion,[33] not puzzled by being presented with a chart they cannot decipher. He is ready, as in the closing song of *The Only Jealousy*, to weight his style and give strength to his imagery with obscure intimations of the philosophy. He does so, though, only when this is theatrically appropriate, as it is in this play for the song of the harlot and the beggar-man. This is detached from the play in the manner of the Noh choruses. It leads away from the event and generalizes the emotion so that the curtain is folded upon a distancing echo, the stage empty and ready to fade into silence. But the song is not the key to the play, which remains stubbornly a matter of interlocked character and plot dramatically realized, and Mr. Wilson, for all his efforts, cannot make it look as if it were. It is only by means of a formidably selective treatment of it that he is able to reach his verdict that 'the play, a play of rejoicing, centres about [Cuchulain's] transfiguration'.[34] This misrepresents the structure of a play in which I see not transfiguration, and certainly not rejoicing—though there is a kind of grim joy in it—but the death of the hero seen as the final irony of his fate.

When Eithne Inguba enters (playing the role assigned to Niamh in Lady Gregory's version) she tells him that she has been charged by Emer to urge him to go forth at once and do battle with the troops of Maeve. Cuchulain is ready, but he notices that Eithne carries a letter in her hand. It is from Emer, and when he reads it he finds that she has written something quite different:

> I am not to move
> Until to-morrow morning, for, if now,
> I must face odds no man can face and live.[35]

In the morning Conall will come to his aid. The discrepancy is explained a few moments later when the Morrigu, goddess of war, appears and stands silently between the pair. Eithne realizes that when she spoke she had been bewitched into acting as the mouthpiece of the goddess, who wishes to destroy Cuchulain. Out of this situation the first episode develops.

Eithne, restored to her faithful self after the trance of deception, cannot save Cuchulain, who is blind to his fate. Although he has Emer's true message, his heart is set upon the grand, heroical gesture, the fight in the face of treachery and against great odds.

This, indeed, is the only right way for a hero of his kind to die, unless he is caught up to heaven by the gods:

> I much prefer
> Your own unwritten words. I am for the fight,
> I and my handful are set upon the fight;
> We have faced great odds before, a straw decided.

Although, by describing Maeve and the Morrigu, Eithne gives him the unmistakable clue that magic is at work, he does not see it, but ascribes the false message to what he thinks is her natural desire to get rid of a lover of whom she is tired. He exclaims in scorn:

> A woman that has an eye in the middle of her forehead!
> A woman that is headed like a crow!

All this, he implies, is fabulous nonsense. But had he not chosen to be blind, he would have recognized the baleful stigmata of the goddess. Despite his conviction that Eithne has sought to betray him, he adopts a role of heroic magnanimity towards her, pointing out how natural her behaviour is in a mistress who longs for a younger man, and how unsurprising, since she failed him in another great crisis, when it was his wife who saved him from the sea. The irony is intensified by his failure to understand that that is precisely what Eithne is trying to do now. Eithne, in despair, accuses him of wanting to die:

> You're not the man I loved,
> That violent man forgave no treachery.
> If, thinking what you think, you can forgive,
> It is because you are about to die.

But he mistakes her horror for exultation at the prospect:

> Spoken too loudly and too near the door;
> Speak low if you would speak about my death,
> Or not in that strange voice exulting in it.
> Who knows what ears listen behind the door?

Eithne cries that, if the servants are listening, at least they won't indulge in this disgusting charade of forgiveness; they have what Cuchulain seems to have lost, 'the passion necessary to life'. When he is dead she will denounce herself for treachery to the 'cooks, scullions, armourers, bed-makers, and messengers'. They are not heroes blinded by their own stories; they will put her to death

> So that my shade can stand among the shades
> And greet your shade and prove it is no traitor.

Cuchulain, unconvinced, answers 'Women have spoken so, plotting a man's death', and his last act before he goes to battle is to ensure that Eithne is drugged in order to prevent her condemning herself, and to charge a servant to 'protect her life As if it were your own'.

It has been necessary to follow the scene in this detailed way in order to show why I cannot see in the episode any sign of a Cuchulain who goes to his last battle in bitterness of heart at Eithne's defection and 'because the death-wish has come upon him'.[36] We have, instead, a dramatization of the reckless energy of the hero, seeking glory in a fight against the odds and behaving with generous forbearance to the woman whom he thinks has tried to bring about his death. Cuchulain of course acknowledges that he may perish in the battle, but he is not, like Lady Gregory's hero, ready to say: 'there is no reason for me to care for my life from this out, for my time is at an end'.[37] That is not the feeling of the scene at all. The 'pardon' granted to Eithne—indeed, the whole elaborate and intimate scene with her—are amongst the material that Yeats did not find in his source and are intended to enhance his portrait of the great-souled man.

The irony, plain to be seen by the audience, derives from the tangle of misunderstandings that is netted about these fine attitudes and drags the hero down. Because his eyes are dazzled by the vision of heroic strife, he cannot recognize the goddess of death standing before him, who makes a doom out of the adventure. Nor can he recognize the faithfulness of Eithne, who has to suffer the worst of horrors in being forgiven for a crime which she has not committed. Cuchulain's end is being determined by his own desire and by his fixed interpretation of his hero's role. The Morrigu is the presiding deity of the play (she claims later to have 'arranged the dance', the dance of death that the drama is, and Emer's dance of mourning that follows it); but, although she presides over the sequences of mortality, she does not directly implement them. Her false message is quickly seen for what it is, even by Cuchulain, who is otherwise incapable of distinguishing the false from the true. Yet plainly, Yeats seems to imply, the hero blinded by the vision of his story, tangled in error and giving those who love him bitter pain, still astonishes us with his majesty.

What is done to this majesty when Cuchulain comes to the moment of dying? The second part of the play is constructed of two antithetical episodes, and the second of these continually looks back towards the first. Cuchulain re-enters, wounded to death. He is followed by Aoife, who has come to kill him, and who helps him to bind himself to the standing-stone so that he may die, like Vespasian and Bussy d'Ambois, upon his feet. The intensely moving dialogue between the masterful, aged Aoife, whose cruelty is full of reminiscent wonder, and Cuchulain, whose voice and rhythms have stilled and melted into the weakness and confusion of the dying, slowly shapes a pattern in which the tragedies of Baile's strand and the hawk's well are remembered. The old story of love mixed with hatred, frustration and tragic error builds up towards what is plainly its one right ending—that Aoife should at last revenge upon his father the death of Conlaoch. Cuchulain admits that she has 'the right to kill me'. 'You have the right', he repeats, and her purpose remains unaltered despite all that they remember of their common history.

But this mounting tension is suddenly diverted; the pattern, just as it is about to become complete, is suddenly abandoned and rubbed out. Aoife's leaving the stage is contrived, awkward, and feebly explained. This is a master-stroke which draws attention to what is being done by the dramatist. It reminds us, with some boldness, as does Shakespeare's occasional use of the technical terms of dramaturgy, that we are in the theatre:

> Somebody comes,
> Some countryman, and when he finds you here,
> And none to protect him, will be terrified.
> I will keep out of his sight, for I have things
> That I must ask questions on before I kill you.

A fine reason for a fine queen to give for the suspension of so vital —or so mortal—a pattern! The Blind Man, who enters now,

81

belongs to that part of the Cuchulain story that owns to ironic commentary on the doings of these great ones:

> Somebody said that I was in Maeve's tent,
> And somebody else, a big man by his voice,
> That if I brought Cuchulain's head in a bag
> I would be given twelve pennies; I had the bag
> To carry what I get at kitchen doors,
> Somebody told me how to find the place;
> I thought it would have taken till the night,
> But this has been my lucky day.

The clown's 'lucky day' is the day on which the hero dies. This, like the final episode in *On Baile's Strand*, is a deliberate trailing of the story in the refuse-dump of 'The Circus Animals' Desertion', the foul rag-and-bone shop of the heart. Cuchulain's own comment is almost his last comment on the heroic adventure, and a total denial of all its glorious rationale:

> Twelve pennies! What better reason for killing a man?

This is an acceptance, but it is not a transfiguration, and Aoife who had all the reason in the heroic world for killing Cuchulain is cheated. The story in which revenge would have meaningfully completed work, life, and death is carefully built up but does not resolve into its climax; the actual ending runs against it. Such is the construction of the play's second part, and it embodies a resounding irony. This is heard again in Cuchulain's vision of his soul after death ('a soft feathery shape . . . a strange shape for the soul / Of a great fighting man'), and in the juxtaposition of our last glimpse of the heroic woman (Emer, as she dances before the severed heads—an episode very dependent upon Lady Gregory's account) with that of the harlot-musician from the street fair.

The Death of Cuchulain is the most majestically designed and the most perfect of the five plays. Yeats has moved a long way from the altogether more obscurely rendered antinomies of *On Baile's Strand*. In the last play he contrived more explicitly than ever before, and with a bold disregard for the timider realisms which it is not absurd to compare with the methods of Shakespeare's last plays, the acting out of the ironies attendant upon the hero's nature and fate. This is done by the characteristic Yeatsian method, which has operated in all the plays, of building up episode against episode and character against character so that the antitheses they form permit the ironic inference to be drawn, or culminate in a moment of revealingly double-natured action: the heroic decision that is also a mistaking (*On Baile's Strand, The Death of Cuchulain*), the love or courage whose expression in action unties the knot one way only to tighten it in another (*The Only Jealousy, At the Hawk's Well*). Yeats's strategy for putting the mythological hero on to the modern stage was cautious and full of ironic reserve in this series of plays. This saved his subject from the Pre-Raphaelite and rhapsodic air that dates the earlier Abbey plays, and from other perishable simplicities, Ossianic or patriotic. But he is never mean or malicious to his hero. and did not permit his audiences to look upon him with a levelling or a rancorous eye or 'pull established honour down'.

Chapter Five

From Grave to Cradle

When all works that have
From cradle run to grave
From grave to cradle run instead.

I

As his discoveries multiplied and his confidence strengthened, Yeats described the condition of the dead with ever greater *ordonnance* and precision. But, although he gradually piled up technical jargon and esoteric detail, this process does not characterize the three plays I am going to discuss in this chapter. They are *The Dreaming of the Bones*, finished in August, 1917, *The Words upon the Window-pane*, finished in October, 1930, and *Purgatory*, begun in March, 1938, and performed at the Abbey in August of the same year.

These plays, written at intervals of about ten years, are at first sight very different from one another, and perhaps they are not commonly thought of together. Of all the Yeatsian Noh plays, *The Dreaming of the Bones* is the one whose form most resembles the traditional Noh of the Ghosts as Yeats read them in the versions of Dr. Stopes, Pound and Fenollosa. *The Words upon the Window-pane*, on the other hand, is a prose one-act play of, for Yeats, a remarkably naturalistic kind, while in *Purgatory* Yeats has invented a form that is largely new. But all three plays set Yeats a similar problem: the intelligible representation of the life of the dead. This was a subject about which he had been speculating with renewed concentration since about 1914. The plays demonstrate Yeats's growing mastery over methods of staging the subject, until he achieves, in *Purgatory*, a success of the first order. It is perhaps his greatest play, and certainly his most profoundly human treatment of this subject.

The plays can mostly be discussed independently of the various discourses in which Yeats worked out his philosophy of death. These discourses belong to a genre different from the theatrical one. Yeats himself was careful not to confuse the two modes; there is nothing in the three plays which is not intelligible even to the uninstructed theatrical spectator, although he may not be aware, if each play is presented to him separately, that each is a fresh attempt at an old theme. The plays do not appear to keep pace with the increasingly elaborate forms taken by the philosophy, though there would be no sense in denying what Yeats himself affirmed: the benefit which his art derived from the growing precision of his thought. 'I find', he wrote to his father at the time when he was composing *The Dreaming of the Bones*, 'the setting of it [the "System"] all in order has helped my verse, has given me a new frame-work and new patterns.'

One goes on year after year gradually getting the disorder of one's mind in order and this is the real impulse to create. Till one has expressed a thing it is like an untidy, unswept, undusted corner of a room.[1]

It would be strange, and would run counter to his own claims for it, if the philosophical mythology had not helped him to practise all his crafts with more elegance and clarity. Sometimes there was muddle which can be attributed to the intrusion of the speculative into the dramatic mode: I have discussed in the previous chapter what seems to be a muddle of this kind in *The Only Jealousy of Emer*.[2] But, considering for how long and how intensely Yeats was obsessed with his speculations, it is extraordinary how deft he became, especially in the works written after *A Vision* was begun, in keeping them to the genres to which they belong: the essay, treatise, gnomic poem, and the few 'texts for exposition'. In this matter he practised a discipline which was never learnt by his master Blake. The kinds of precision characteristic of the Yeatsian system—diagrams, classifications, formulae, technical terms, and citations from authorities—were utterly different from those which a drama requires in order to conform to its own mode of being: setting, costume, movement, speech, and the needs of actors. A glimpse into the systematized thought may show what it was that the barriers of the drama stood firm against, and will serve to introduce the themes common to the three plays.

There are four principal prose-writings in which Yeats wrought into system his ideas on the life of the dead. These are, in the order of their composition, the essay entitled 'Swedenborg, Mediums, and the Desolate Places', which was written about 1914 and printed in Lady Gregory's *Visions and Beliefs in the West of Ireland* (1920); the 'Anima Mundi' section of the treatise entitled *Per Amica Silentia Lunae* (1918); and a portion in each of the editions of *A Vision*: Book IV ('The Gates of Pluto') in the edition of 1925, and Book III ('The Soul in Judgment') in the edition of 1937. The essay in Lady Gregory's collection is a jumble, but it cites the authorities that Yeats was busy collating with his own spiritualistic experiences in castle and cottage. They include Plato, the neo-Platonists (Plotinus, Porphyry, Proclus, Synesius, Philoponus), the Cambridge Platonists (Henry More, Glanvil, Cudworth, Joseph Beaumont), Swedenborg, Allen Cardec and Jackson Davis (French and American Swedenborgians), numerous modern writers on psychical research (in a note Yeats mentions a dozen names), the Noh Ghost plays in the Pound / Fenollosa versions, Irish folk-lore, and the 'fat old woman', a medium in Soho, who would 'tell in Cockney language how the dead do not yet know they are dead'.[3] In *Per Amica* some of these names recur, but Yeats has purged his text of much of the confusion which they had wrought in the earlier essay. He now adopts a more personal and dogmatic approach to the subject, a style richer in metaphor and allusion. The obscurity here is of a different kind: an argument is not unfolded; it is glimpsed by snatches. Twenty-two brief numbered sections behave like detached meditations, *pensées* flying off at a tangent from one another. The allusiveness is not designed to persuade the intellect of the truth of what is being said but to lead us to an 'O altitudo' whereby judgement is suspended. Here, for example, is section xii in its entirety:

The dead living in their memories, are, I am persuaded, the source of all that we call instinct, and it is their love and their desire, all unknow-

86

ing, that make us drive beyond our reason, or in defiance of our interest it may be; and it is the dream martens that, all unknowing, are mastermasons to the living martens building about church windows their elaborate nests; and in their turn, the phantoms are stung to a keener delight from a concord between their luminous pure vehicle and our strong senses. It were to reproach the power or the beneficence of God, to believe those children of Alexander, who died wretchedly, could not throw an urnful to the heap, nor Caesarion murdered in childhood, whom Cleopatra bore to Caesar, nor the brief-lived younger Pericles Aspasia bore—being so nobly born.[4]

The criteria for such a passage are those applicable to the prosepoem, and in general *Per Amica* is as much about the prose-poet's emotion as he contemplates the profundity and grandeur of it all as about the subject itself. The 'untidy room' has not been swept; instead Yeats exults in its rich confusion.

It is not until 'The Gates of Pluto' and its second version in the second edition of *A Vision* that Yeats shakes himself free of the cloud of witnesses and his own crowding emotions. In writing *A Vision* he was experimenting with yet another genre, which is characterized by the use of technical vocabulary. This was not a complete innovation, because technical terms had appeared here and there in the two preceding documents, but in *A Vision* it is the essential manner of proceeding. Contrast, for example, this passage from 'The Gates of Pluto' with the passage I have just quoted from *Per Amica*:

The *Spirit* first floats horizontally within the man's dead body, but then rises until it stands at his head. The *Celestial Body* is also horizontal at first but lies in the opposite position, its feet where the *Spirit's* head is, and then rising, as does the *Spirit*, stands up at last at the feet of the man's body. The *Passionate Body* rises straight up from the genitals and stands in the centre. The *Husk* remains in the body until the time for it to be separated and lost in the *Anima Mundi*. The separation of the *Principles* from the body is caused by the *Daimon's* gathering into the *Passionate Body* memory of the past life—perhaps but a single image or thought—which is always taken from the unconscious memories of the living, from the *Record* of all those things which have been seen but have not been noticed or accepted by the intellect, and the *Record* is always truthful.[5]

This is entirely dogmatic and arbitrary, but internally coherent.

87

It makes use of terms which often have the opalescence of poetic imagery but do not shift their meaning when once they have been defined. In *A Vision* Yeats has found a form to match his thought. It is that of the metaphysical treatise, part Plotinian, part Swedenborgian. It was the right form. If you think like Swedenborg or Plotinus, then you might as well write like them too. The other documents in the case are a learned essay obfuscated by its anxiety about authorities, and a 'Religio Poetae' which cannot do justice to the System's conceptual elements because it is continually distracted by poetic excitement.

From this point of view, then, it is fair to describe the evolution of the System, in so far as it bears upon Yeats's beliefs about the condition of the dead, as a choice amongst kinds. All of them are, however, far distant from the dramatic kind, and the choice that proved most successful—the neo-Plotinian treatise—is the furthest away of all. Although they have a root in the one mind, the forms through which the thought of the System evolves and grows clearer is a branch which springs continually away from that other branch, the three ghost-plays and *their* formal evolution. There is no sense in which the plays are transcriptions of the documents that I have discussed. If comparison there is to be, it must take place at a point below that from which the disparate branches spring; and if transcription there was, it took the form of two different transcriptions of a common theme, which afterwards developed, in the prose-treatises and in the plays, two different ways of living.

As it is stated in the first of the prose documents, 'Swedenborg, Mediums, and the Desolate Places', this common theme has already become much more minutely detailed than it is in the earliest of the plays, *The Dreaming of the Bones*, although Yeats was able in his prose-note on that play to put it precisely enough as 'the world-wide belief that the dead dream back, for a certain time, through the more personal thoughts and deeds of life'.[6] So in 'Swedenborg, Mediums, and the Desolate Places', the dead live 'an earth-resembling life [which] is the creation of the image-making power of the mind, plucked naked from the body, and mainly of the images in the memory':[7]

All spirits for some time after death, and the 'earth-bound', as they are called, the larvae, as Beaumont, the seventeenth-century Platonist,

88

preferred to call them, those who cannot become disentangled from old habits and desires, for many years, it may be for centuries, keep the shape of their earthly bodies and carry on their old activities, wooing or quarrelling, or totting figures on a table, in a round of dull duties or passionate events.[8]

Per Amica uses again some of the picturesque examples of this state which had been cited in *Visions and Beliefs*:[9]

Spiritism, whether of folk-lore or of the séance-room, the visions of Swedenborg, and the speculations of the Platonists and Japanese plays, will have it that we may see at certain roads and in certain houses old murders acted over again, and in certain fields dead huntsmen riding with horse and hound, or ancient armies fighting above bones or ashes.[10]

The dead, declares Yeats, must not be thought of as 'living an abstract life for it is the living who create abstraction which "consumes itself away" '.[11] Their condition, as they live through the passionate events, is ever more clearly seen as one of purgatorial expiation: 'the toil of the living is to free themselves from an endless sequence of objects, and that of the dead to free themselves from an endless sequence of thoughts':[12]

The dead, as the passionate necessity wears out, come into a measure of freedom . . . gradually they perceive, although they are still but living in their memories, harmonies, symbols, and patterns, as though all were being refashioned by an artist, and they are moved by emotions, sweet for no imagined good but in themselves, like those of children dancing in a ring; and I do not doubt that they make love in that union which Swedenborg has said is of the whole body and seems from far off an incandescence.[13]

The expiatory condition is one of several stages of purification in the first edition of *A Vision*, and is there described with a comparative absence of technicalities:

it is now that, according to ancient and modern tradition, the murderer may be seen committing his murder night after night or perhaps upon the anniversary of its first committal; . . . or it may be that the dream is happy and that the seer but meets the old huntsman hunting once more amid a multitude of his friends . . . the man must dream the event to its consequence as far as his intensity permit; not that consequence only which occurred while he lived, and was known to him, but those that were unknown, or have occurred after his death. The more complete the exploration, the more fortunate will be his future life, but he is concerned with events only, and with the emotions that accompanied events. Every event so dreamed is the expression of some knot, some concentration of feeling separating off a period of time, or portion of the being, from the being as a whole and the life as a whole, and the dream is as it were a smoothing out or an unwinding. Yet it is said that if his nature had great intensity, and the consequence of the event affected multitudes, he may dream with slowly lessening pain and joy for centuries.[14]

In the second edition of *A Vision* this passage has disappeared to make way for bleaker categories and more complex distinctions.

This indicates the character and some of the details of the theme which the three plays have in common. Elizabethan plays had their ghosts, but in the hard task of giving theatrical life to the dead, Yeats could not follow that example.

II

He went, indeed, to quite another tradition for *The Dreaming of the Bones* and sought a model in the type of Noh play which dramatizes the 'meeting with ghost, god, or goddess at some holy place or much-legended tomb', the supernatural stories which reminded him of 'our own Irish legends and beliefs'.[15]

A young revolutionary soldier, in flight from the enemy after the Easter Rising, comes to a desolate, hilly place on the borders of Galway and Clare. There he encounters the shades of Dermot and Dervorgilla, who 'brought the Norman in'.[16] They are imprisoned in their own remorse, punished by longing for each other but held from union by the memory of their crime. Gradually they reveal their identity to the soldier and tell him how their pain can be relieved:

> They were not wholly miserable and accursed
> If somebody of their race at last would say:
> 'I have forgiven them.' [17]

But the soldier cannot forgive them, and the play ends with their dance of unappeased longing.

In 1917 Yeats thought that this was 'the best play I have written for years', and he was still enthusiastic about it fourteen years later.[18] Yeats has successfully learnt the lesson of the Noh as it was taught by Fenollosa, with its emphasis on intensity and purity of a kind that might well appeal to the author of *Deirdre*.

The beauty and power of Noh lie in the concentration. All elements—costume, motion, verse, and music—unite to produce a single clarified impression. Each drama embodies some primary human relation or emotion; and the poetic sweetness or poignancy of this is carried to its highest degree by carefully excluding all such obtrusive elements as a mimetic realism or vulgar sensation might demand. . . . Now it is brotherly love, now love to a parent, now loyalty to a master, love of husband and wife, of mother for a dead child, or of jealousy or anger, of self-mastery in battle, of the battle of passion itself, of the clinging of a ghost to the scene of its sin, of the infinite compassion of a Buddha, of the sorrow of unrequited love. Some one of these intense emotions is chosen for a piece, and, in it, elevated to the plane of universality by the intensity and purity of treatment.[19]

This concentration and unity of mood is more noticeable in *The Dreaming of the Bones* than in any of the Yeatsian Noh plays discussed in the preceding chapter. It is achieved by imagery, by the description of setting and locale, and by construction.

In his essay on the Noh plays Yeats claimed to have detected in the examples with which he was familiar 'a playing upon a single metaphor, as deliberate as the echoing rhythm of line in Chinese and Japanese painting'.[20] In *The Dreaming of the Bones* it is the hour before dawn. Yeats uses an iterative image-cluster which evokes the sounds of the haunted night and holds them in contrast against the longed-for crowing of the cock that heralds the coming of the day. In the Musicians' speech and songs appear the birds that 'cry in their loneliness', the 'tomb-nested owl', the 'cat-headed bird' crying out in the shadow below the hills.

> The dreaming bones cry out
> Because the night winds blow

and the 'music of a lost kingdom', a wandering, airy music 'heard in the night air',

> Runs, runs and is suddenly still.
> The winds out of Clare-Galway
> Carry it: suddenly it is still.

These sounds contrast with the crowing of the cocks, bringing danger to the soldier and dismissal to the shades, as in the refrain of the Musicians' song:

> Red bird of March, begin to crow,
> Up with the neck and clap the wing,
> Red cock, and crow,

and spilling over into several allusions in the dialogue. Finally, this cluster of images appears as a coda in the last lines of the play.

Another controlling and unifying device is the detailed evocation of the setting amidst 'cold Clare rock and Galway rock and thorn'. The setting is more specific and the use of place-names more generous than in any of the other Yeatsian Noh plays, and closest to *The King's Threshold*. But, according to Yeats, he had improved on that play with the help of his Japanese models and the example of the emotion felt by the Japanese poets for 'tomb and wood', which he compared to the 'sense of awe that our Gaelic-speaking country people will sometimes show when you speak to them of Castle Hackett or of some Holy Well'.[21] And so the play is steeped in the sense of place, of rocks, ruined abbey, and the view over town, islands, and sea.

It is divided, like many of the Japanese Noh plays themselves, into two portions, separated by an interlude during which the shades guide the soldier to the hill-top where he is to watch for the boat that comes to take him away to safety. But the unification of the episodes depends upon the way the ghosts gradually reveal their identity and the nature of their suffering. As in *Nishikigi*, the ghosts tell their story but 'they do not say at first that it is their own story' (Fenollosa).[22] As in that play, the traveller does not seem to notice their ancient attire or their heroic masks. This is perhaps because at first the scene is dark—a darkness imaginatively rendered by the blowing out of the soldier's lantern. During the first episode he learns first that the place is haunted, and by a particular variety of spiritual being: those who must 'live through their old lives again'. More is slowly unfolded during the second episode. The shade of Dermot alludes to Donogh O'Brien, buried in the ruined graveyard; he

> rebelled against the King of Thomond
> And died in his youth.

But the crime for which *these* spirits suffer is much more hateful than rebellion, and because of it they are confined to an accursed solitude. Not until the whole story of Dermot and Dervorgilla has been recalled and the two phantoms begin to re-enact their agony in the final dance does the soldier realize, as the light of dawn breaks over Galway, who his guides have been:

> Why do you dance?
> Why do you gaze, and with so passionate eyes,
> One on the other; and then turn away,
> Covering your eyes, and weave it in a dance?
> Who are you? what are you?

To end the play with the dance of the unappeased shades was to imitate *Motomezuka*, one of the Noh plays to which Yeats refers most often. His own words are: 'Instead of the disordered passion of nature there is a dance, a series of positions and movements which may represent a battle, or a marriage, or the pain of a ghost in the Buddhist purgatory.'[23]

It was, then, by a fairly faithful transposition into an Irish key of some of the devices that he most valued in the Noh that Yeats dramatized the supernatural life in this play. The particular phase of the discarnate life that Dermot and Dervorgilla are caught in can be identified, if we wish to do so, from documents other than the play itself.* But a gloss of this kind is not really needed for *The Dreaming of the Bones*. Yeats supplied in the text itself all of

---

* According to the second edition of *A Vision* (the classifications are somewhat altered from the first edition), there can be three states in the second stage of the life of the discarnate spirit: the *Dreaming Back*, the *Return*, and the *Phantasmagoria*. The last is distinguished from the first two partly by its being 'self-created' by the spirit, which undergoes during it emotional suffering due to remorse for sin committed in life (*A Vision*, 1937 edn., pp. 225-31). The punishments which it must live through are its 'own conscience made visible' (*A Vision*, 1925, p. 225). This phase must be exhausted before the spirit can proceed to the next stage. Dermot and Dervorgilla seem to belong to this phase, and it is linked with them in that Yeats should so often have cited as an example of the phase the sufferings of the spectre in *Motomezuka* which is 'set afire by a fantastic scruple, and though a Buddhist priest explains that the fire would go out of itself if the ghost but ceased to believe in it, it cannot cease to believe' (*Per Amica, Essays*, 1924, p. 521: compare the places cited from *A Vision* above, as well as *Visions and Beliefs*, II. 334 and *Four Plays for Dancers*, p. 129).

his thought that was theatrically viable and all that was needed to
render the condition of the ghosts moving and intelligible:

> These have no thought but love; nor joy
> But that upon the instant when their penance
> Draws to its height and when two hearts are wrung
> Nearest to breaking, if hearts of shadows break,
> His eyes can mix with hers; nor any pang
> That is so bitter as that double glance,
> Being accursed . . .[24]
>> when he has bent his head
> Close to her head, or hand would slip in hand,
> The memory of their crime flows up between
> And drives them apart.[25]

Nor did Yeats spoil the completeness of his tragic form by representing the life of his spirits as only one amongst many stages of
discarnate existence. That type of distinction belongs to the mode
of the neo-Plotinian treatise rather than of the drama. The soldier's
forgiveness, had it been granted, could only have mitigated their
suffering not ended it. Even if some act of forgiveness had made
possible the passionate union of the shades, their union would not
at all have corresponded to the *Shiftings*, the third discarnate stage,
to which the ghosts, if they had been conforming to *A Vision*,
might have proceeded.

But peace and reconciliation amongst the dead, brought about
by the intervention of the living, would have been a peripeteia in
no way alien to the Noh tradition itself. One thinks of the priest's
prayer in *Nishikigi* and the union of dead lovers that follows it, or
of the exorcists in *Awoi No Uye* who drive the demon away and
bring the dead woman peace. It would not have been foreign to
Yeats's own art either, as 'Ribh at the Tomb of Baile and Aillinn'
and its various analogues bear witness. That no event of this kind
happens in *The Dreaming of the Bones* is due to its basic conception,
and draws attention to the important element in its construction
that has yet to be discussed.

In *The Dreaming of the Bones* there is a political element which
at first sight seems incongruous. Yeats made somewhat worried
mention of it in a letter to Lady Gregory and elsewhere.[26] The
play is timed just after the Easter Rising, and there are many

references to war and destruction. When he sees the dispossessed and ruined abbey the soldier exclaims:

> Is there no house
> Famous for sanctity or architectural beauty
> In Clare or Kerry, or in all wide Connacht
> The enemy has not unroofed?

The soldier himself is a somewhat surprising substitute for the neutral intercessor to whom in the Noh plays ghosts often manifest themselves. But the point that Yeats is making is clear enough. The hunted patriot and the destruction everywhere must be recognized as the direct consequences of the sin committed seven centuries ago:

> What generations of old men had known
> Like their own hands, and children wondered at,
> Has boiled a trooper's porridge. That town had lain,
> But for the pair that you would have me pardon,
> Amid its gables and its battlements
> Like any old admired Italian town.

The enemy whom the soldier fights is that same 'foreign army from across the sea' which Dermot and Dervorgilla 'brought in'. The Easter Rising, one of those occasions which fans the sequel of continuous misery into a disastrous blaze, may be supposed to aggravate the torment of conscience in which the lovers have 'lost themselves'. They are like the girl in *Motomezuka*, whose 'Ghost tells a Priest of a slight sin which seems a great sin because of its unforeseen and unforeseeable consequences'[27] (in her case the suicide of a rejected lover); or like the ghost in *A Vision* who must 'dream the event to its consequence'.[28]

But there is no suggestion in the play that intenser consequence and sharper suffering are, as they are in *A Vision*, a purgatorial therapy which will smooth out and unwind the pain. In this way the play folds in upon itself. The antique story is tied to the present moments of flight and disaster because they proceed from it; the lovers inhabit a landscape of ruin which they made themselves; they address their hopeless appeal to the traveller whom, as revolutionary and fugitive, they fathered. There is, as it were, no room for a peripeteia. The soldier himself is caught inside this tight circle; he is one of the consequences of their transgression and cannot forgive the authors of the evil which he fights and curses.

It is of him, however, that they ask forgiveness. This introduces at the end of the play a moral dilemma, an element entailing a choice and a possible development therefrom. These are things which the play's construction and the soldier's inherited role otherwise preclude.

It is not easy to decide whether this modifies the design of *The Dreaming of the Bones* in the wrong way. It seems to be in accord with Yeats's thought that the remorse of the dead may be lessened by some intervention on the part of those descendants of the dead man who have been affected by unforeseen consequences of his original crime. This is a theme which Yeats was to explore in *Purgatory*, although I do not know of anywhere else in his writings where it is explicitly treated. In *The Dreaming of the Bones* forgiveness is the intervention proposed. During the spirits' dance of agony the soldier does nearly forgive them:

> I had almost yielded and forgiven all—
> This is indeed a place of terrible temptation.

This moment certainly increases the tension at the end of the play, and this perhaps is its justification. But it does so at the cost of introducing inconsistency into the soldier's role. Throughout—although it is to him that the tale is told—he is never, except on this occasion, a mediator. He neither experiences nor transmits to the audience anything resembling pity or horror at the ghosts' fate. He is preoccupied with flight, danger, and hatred:

> It was men like Donogh that made Ireland weak—
> My curse on all that troop.

The dramatic method, too, has been to arouse pity and horror in the audience directly and not through his mediation, by what the ghosts say and the musicians shudder at, and not by what the soldier feels about what he hears.

Thus the soldier's moment of 'almost yielding' in some ways intensifies the theme by offering and then withdrawing a hope of relief, and so brings out still more cruelly the necessity imposed upon the shades of living through the old round unassuaged. But in other ways it makes for incongruity by allowing us to glimpse beyond this play a play with a different structure, one which admits both a purgatory and a peripeteia. This flaw, if it is one, detracts very little from a design that is moving because of its coherence, interlocking crime and consequence so that everything becomes intense and clear.

III

But *The Dreaming of the Bones*, which pleased Yeats perhaps because he had finally mastered the Noh models in begetting its autonomous life upon them, cannot have satisfied him entirely. Its mode of existence is closer to that of the lyrical poem than are the Noh plays which preceded it and followed it. In these, *At the Hawk's Well* and *The Only Jealousy of Emer*, there is found the untying of the knot by some movement of action which resolved a crisis and settled Cuchulain's or Emer's destiny. In *The Dreaming of the Bones* nothing is done or undone, and scarcely anything disturbs the intensity with which suffering winds in upon itself. The play is the nearest of the three to that 'pure presentation of the image in the theatre' which Frank Kermode sees as the rationale of all Yeats's adaptations of the Noh.[29] *The Words upon the Window-pane* is some sort of evidence that Yeats wanted to work in other modes as well, and it falls into place here because it also dramatizes the discarnate life.

Yeats had much experience of séances. The period between 1911 and 1916 seems to have been specially active. During those years the unpublished notebooks record details of many sessions and the work of many mediums.[30] In the introduction to *The Words upon the Window-pane* he declared that all the people in it 'were people I had met or might have met in just such a séance'.[31]

The scene is a Dublin lodging-house where six people are assembling for a séance with a visiting medium from London. Three of them, Corny Patterson, Mrs. Mallet, and the Reverend Abraham Johnson, are slyly amusing caricatures of typical addicts. Then there is the secretary of the group, Miss Mackenna, Dr. Trench, its president, and John Corbet, a visitor from Cambridge, who is writing a thesis on Swift. The house in which they find themselves had once belonged to friends of Swift's Stella; Trench shows Corbet the lines from Stella's birthday-poem to Swift

97

which have been cut upon the window-pane, and they discuss the tragedy of Swift's personal life. The other characters, meanwhile, speak of what they hope for from the séance—news about heaven, advice from the late Mr. Mallet, the spiritual inspiration of Sankey and Moody—and allude to the way in which these expectations have been disappointed in preceding séances by the unwanted presence of two spirits who have gone through 'the same drama' on each occasion 'as if they were characters in some kind of horrible play'. Dr. Trench echoes Yeats's own thoughts when he speaks of earth-bound spirits who

think they are still living and go over and over some action of their past lives, just as we go over and over some painful thought, except that where they are thought is reality . . . if I were a Catholic I would say that such spirits were in Purgatory.[32]

The grotesque and the mysteriously painful are very dexterously combined in the protasis. Its themes are developed in the central episode of the play and help to make it intelligible. Here the medium, Mrs. Henderson, speaks in the voices of Lulu (her 'control'), of Swift, and of Vanessa. Between Vanessa and Swift the 'horrible play' is played through again: Swift's fear and loathing of procreation struggling with Vanessa's avowal of love and culminating in his terrible cry of 'who locked me in with my enemy?' This is followed by the calm of the spirit's long monologue addressed to Stella, in whom he seeks and thinks he finds moral assuagement and friendship for old age. The medium emerges exhausted from her trance; one by one the disappointed spiritualists file away, and the end of the play comes in sight.

To the effectiveness of the play on the stage there is testimony, although one wonders how many actresses would be equal to the part of Mrs. Henderson. Of the blending together in its structure of the story of the séance and the story of Swift and the tensions created by that method A. N. Jeffares has written perceptively.[33] I want to add some further thoughts about the way it is constructed and to consider the play in company with *The Dreaming of the Bones*.

'An excellent play about Swift'[34] has been the commentators' verdict, and it was as a play about Swift that Yeats referred to it in his letters. The choice of Swift as central figure arose from

Yeats's new interest in the eighteenth century—the 'one Irish century that escaped from darkness and confusion'.[35] But in the play these representative qualities of Swift (which are considered at length in its Introduction) get very little mention. Into its dramatic centre Yeats put instead the darkness and confusion of Swift's private life, and we are presented with an image of discarnate suffering which has the completeness and the same kind of infolded structure as *The Dreaming of the Bones*. Nor is the resemblance between the two plays much modified by the fact that the author of *A Vision* would have distinguished quite sharply between the shades in the earlier play 'caught in a winding labyrinth of conscience' and those in the later, who are re-living, as Dr. Trench explains, 'some passionate or tragic moment of life. . . . In vain do we write *requiescat in pace* upon the tomb, for they must suffer, and we in our turn must suffer until God gives peace.' The choice of a famous historical figure to play the role of suffering spirit is justified as much by the naturalistic Dublin setting as by an interest in Swift for its own sake. There is a sense in which anyone else whose life could yield the necessary perturbations would have done. But, having chosen Swift, Yeats was sufficiently obedient to the naturalistic tradition to provide all the realism of content that, within that tradition, makes for theatrical life.

There is also affinity with *The Dreaming of the Bones* in the final phase of the play. The last words of the shade of Swift are 'Yes, you will close my eyes, Stella. O you will live long after me, dear Stella, for you are still a young woman, but you will close my eyes.' After the others have gone, Corbet, the expert on Swift, who is unconvinced that anything he has heard has been the work of spirits, attributes to Mrs. Henderson a knowledge as great or greater than his own and tries to discuss Swift with her:

MRS. HENDERSON

Swift? I do not know anybody called Swift.

JOHN CORBET

Jonathan Swift, whose spirit seemed to be present to-night.

MRS. HENDERSON

What? That dirty old man?

99

JOHN CORBET

He was neither old nor dirty when Stella and Vanessa loved him.

MRS. HENDERSON

I saw him very clearly just as I woke up. His clothes were dirty, his face covered with boils. Some disease had made one of his eyes swell up, it stood out from his face like a hen's egg.

JOHN CORBET

He looked like that in his old age. Stella had been dead a long time. His brain had gone, his friends had deserted him.*

This conversation completes the Swiftian tragedy and makes a self-subsistent image out of it. The words upon the window-pane ('Late dying, may you cast a shred / Of that rich mantle o'er my head'), the prediction that Stella will close Swift's eyes, the flight to Stella for a refuge from his 'enemy' Vanessa and from the perilous consequences and responsibilities of physical love—these hopes are now seen to have been false and to have led only to madness and despair. By balancing the Stella episode against the conversation of John Corbet with Mrs. Henderson, Yeats completes his structure, and completes it with an irony comparable with that in *The Dreaming of the Bones*. The moment of appeasement represented by the communion with Stella resembles the relief that the lovers in the earlier play hope for from the pardon for which they ask the soldier. In *The Dreaming of the Bones* the soldier, as 'unforeseen consequence' of their sin, is a part of what torments the shades. So, too, in *The Words upon the Window-pane*, Stella herself is only a part of the lonely ghost's memories. Her voicelessness is significant; she is not present, as Vanessa is, and does not speak, as Vanessa does, through the medium, presumably because her spirit has long ago proceeded to some purer stage of

* We must infer, I think, that Yeats imagined that all the 'dreaming-back' recorded through the medium's mouth earlier in the play was the activity of the shade not of the younger Swift, of the same age as he was when the events took place in his life, but of the old, mad, deserted Swift. In old age he is imagined as dwelling on his memories, and these memories were the painful thoughts that were the substance of his madness. In death, therefore, his shade assumes this form and relives those painful thoughts. The ghost in the play is the equivalent of the mind of the mad, older Swift. Lulu refers to the shade, even during the Vanessa episode, as a 'bad *old* man', and his physical form, as glimpsed by Mrs. Henderson, is that of the aged Swift.

the discarnate life. She cannot pardon or release; Swift, like the bride in *Purgatory*, is 'alone in [his] remorse'.[36] The condition of the ghost's life is that he must live through the whole round of his painful thoughts that are his memories and may not find a place to stay and hide in any one of them. In a similar fashion, the continual consciousness of their sin is the condition of the life of the dead in *The Dreaming of the Bones*. But, as not in that play, there is in this one a hint from the author of *A Vision* (through the mouth of Dr. Trench)[37] that all this pain is expiatory and will pass away. It is a hint so slight that it does little to impair the cruel integrity of the tragic image.

There is a final twist of the knife, or pinnacle added to the construction, after Corbet leaves the stage. Yeats stretches the naturalistic mode by giving Mrs. Henderson what almost amounts to a soliloquy. The exhausted medium, trying to make herself a cup of tea, speaks suddenly in Swift's voice again and uses, amongst others, words recorded as having been spoken during his insanity: 'Perish the day on which I was born!' These are the last words of the play. As the only direct address to the audience in the play, the theatrical effect is all the greater. It deliberately shocks the audience into casting its mind back over the rationale of the whole affair.[38]

We know something of how Yeats would have explained Mrs. Henderson's last actions, because he tells us in his Introduction, warning us at the same time that he has not put this explanation into the play. Mediumship, he writes, is dramatization. The medium works like the actor by creating a 'secondary personality':

Perhaps May Craig [the actress who played Mrs. Henderson], when alone in her room after the play, went, without knowing what she was doing, through some detail of her performance. I once saw an Abbey actor going up the stairs to his dressing-room after playing the part of a lame man and saw that he was still limping.[39]

I do not fully understand the pages in which this idea is worked out, but Yeats is not, I think, doubting that in certain cases and under certain conditions the spirits of the dead many manifest themselves at mediumistic séances. The method by which the medium, whether false or genuine, works is the same. The difference between the false and the genuine is comparable, perhaps, to the difference between the bad actor who fakes and the good actor who conveys the reality in his part. By this reading, therefore, Mrs. Henderson's final actions need not cast any doubt upon the actuality of the shades or suggest that she is, as John Corbet supposes, 'an accomplished actress and scholar', except in so far as every medium is, in Yeats's view, an actress, a dramatizer, more or less accomplished.

But since the explanation that Yeats supplies in the Introduction is carefully excluded from the play itself, the audience is left to its own deductions. Because the dramatist has so provided, these will be mostly sceptical. The favourite one is likely to be, not that Mrs. Henderson is a mere fraud, but that she has been the unconscious receiver and dramatizer of the thoughts of John Corbet, the Swift scholar, whose somewhat obtrusive presence in the play seems designed to foster just such a conclusion. And even when he has left the stage she is still, in her exhausted state, subject to his influence, his last ruminations about Swift as he leaves the house. This type of event was accepted by Yeats as likely enough to occur during a séance.* Nor need Yeats's own explanation in the Introduction of Mrs. Henderson's last speech at all exclude the possibility that something of the kind has happened. There is always in mediumship a 'secondary personality' and several different ways in which it can be begotten. That traces of it cling to the dramatizing medium after the show is over can tell us nothing about the genuineness or otherwise of the show itself.

Yet the play is so designed that it is impossible to rest in this scepticism. It has been carefully indicated in the protasis that Corbet is now attending for the first time, that there have been three previous séances, and that the last two have both been spoilt by the 'horrible play' in which Swift and Vanessa have gone through the same drama and said the same words. We are set wondering again. Is the room in which Stella played cards and cut her verses on the window-pane truly revisited by her lover's shade? Do Mrs.

---

* He speaks in the Introduction of an occasion when 'the mind of an old doting general [one of the sitters] turned all to delirium', and in *Per Amica* writes of spirits who transmit through a medium finding it difficult to 'speak their own thoughts and keep their own memory . . . [they] readily mistake our memory for their own, and believe themselves whom and what we please. We bewilder and overmaster them' (*Essays*, 1924, p. 531).

Henderson's last words mean that she is still subject to the revenant, and is likely to be as long as she remains in the haunted house? The audience is deliberately left uncertain, in a frame of mind which corresponds to that of Miss Mackenna and of Yeats himself:

I have seen a good many séances, and sometimes think it is all coincidence and thought-transference. . . . Then at other times I think as Dr. Trench does, and then I feel like Job—you know the quotation—the hair of my head stands up. A spirit passes before my face.

In dramatizing the modern séance-room Yeats was forced to adopt the naturalistic mode. He seems to calculate the expectations that his audience will bring to a play about this subject, and avoids what might have been a temptation inherent in it: the writing of a tract for or against spiritualism. In the manner of a problem-play dramatist he keeps his audience's intellectual faculties working, but also in presenting the completed tragedy of Swift he endeavours to move it as he had in *The Dreaming of the Bones*. Yeats has made a finished image of suffering and set about it a naturalistic problem-play on spiritualism. It is in this sense that it is a 'play about Swift'.

IV

' "And another time I saw Purgatory. It seemed to be in a level place, and no walls around it, but it all in one bright blaze, and the souls standing in it. And they suffer near as much as in Hell, only there are no devils with them there, and they have the hope of Heaven." ' So spoke the old Galway villager, commemorated in *The Celtic Twilight*, 'who can see nothing but wickedness. Some think him very holy, and others think him a little crazed.' [40] For his last play on this theme Yeats chose an image which goes back to his younger years, to Castle Dargan, and the 'ruined castle lit up'.[41] From a ghost-story that Yeats himself told, about a family ruined by drink, a castle burnt down, and an 'ashen woman' repeatedly seen by her descendants living through her act of suicide, Yeats borrowed other main themes for *Purgatory*,[42] weaving the diffuseness of the old story into a tight dramatic narrative. The shades in this play, haunting the ruined mansion, are nearer to the audience than the mythological and historical figures of Dermot, Dervorgilla, and Swift, because they derive from the popular tale.

The scene is 'a ruined house and a bare tree in the background'.[43] A wandering pedlar and his bastard son stand in the moonlight before the ruin, while the old man reveals its history to the boy. In this house the pedlar had been born, the son of a great lady who had married a drunken groom. After his wife's death in child-birth, the groom had squandered the estate, but his son had been taught to read and had got a haphazard education. The boy listens enviously to the tale of riches and learning. When the old man was sixteen, the groom had burned down the house in a drunken frenzy and his son had stabbed him to death in the ruins and fled to escape trial. When this exposition is finished, the action begins.

It is the anniversary of the mother's wedding-night. Her remorseful shade must act the occasion through again and again, tortured by her knowledge of the ruinous consequences of her marriage. The old man hears the hoof-beats of the bridegroom's horse on the gravelled drive, and the figure of the bride appears at a lighted window of the ruin. The boy his son, meanwhile, can see and hear nothing, and mockingly accuses the old man of madness. A long speech from the old man divides the play into two portions, as he describes the wedding-night, cries out vainly to his mother's shade 'Do not let him touch you!', and meditates on the mystery of her re-enactment of the sexual act. But his meditation is interrupted by the boy, who had seized the chance of stealing the bag of money from the pedlar's pack and is making off with it. The catastrophe approaches in intensifying violence.

They struggle for the money, which is scattered on the ground, and the boy threatens to kill his father. While this is going on, the figure of the bridegroom appears at the window, leaning there like 'a tired beast'. The boy can see this apparition;* as, filled with horror, he hides his eyes, the old man stabs him to death. The window in which the apparition stands now darkens,

---

* The boy can see this second apparition perhaps because he, like his grandfather the groom, represents the evil, degenerate element in the family-story. He cannot see the apparition of his grandmother because his evil nature cannot 'dramatize' it.

and it seems as if the phantom, the 'nothing' that is the 'impression on my mother's mind', has been exorcized. Another stage-effect (which is seen to be equally ironic when the true catastrophe occurs, follows: the dry tree that emblematized when it was green the rich life of the prosperous family now appears bathed in white light on the darkened stage. As the old man looks at it standing there 'like a purified soul' he explains why he killed the boy. It was to put an end to the chain of consequence, the polluted blood that would have 'Begot, and passed pollution on'. As he bends to pick up the scattered money, the bridegroom's hoof-beats are heard again. The old man realizes in despair that the dream of the dead woman cannot come to an end:

> Twice a murderer and all for nothing,
> And she must animate that dead night
> Not once but many times!

The play ends with his prayer to God to release the tormented soul from its dream, for 'Mankind can do no more'.

In this play, the conscience of the shade compels her to re-enact her transgression at that moment when it initiated the chain of consequence that fills her with remorse: the begetting of a child. This is the knot the old man strives to cut. The souls in Purgatory, he says, that 'come back to habitations and familiar spots'

> know at last
> The consequence of those transgressions
> Whether upon others or upon themselves;
> Upon others, others may bring help,
> For when the consequence is at an end
> The dream must end; upon themselves,
> There is no help but in themselves
> And in the mercy of God.

The consequence of her crime upon 'others' that is most vividly presented in the play is the dynastic one, represented especially by the character of the boy. He is ignorant, amoral, thieving, a potential parricide, and—it is hinted—lecher. The boy, then, is to be killed, to be 'exorcized' like the grandfather, and the degenerate stock wiped out. Otherwise, he will repeat the pattern of his polluted father's career, which began at sixteen, the boy's age, with the murder of the groom, and went on to the begetting of a bastard 'Upon a tinker's daughter in a ditch'. And so on to generations unborn. When the boy is killed, the mother's spirit is momentarily assuaged. This is emblematized by the tree's becoming 'like a purified soul':

> All cold, sweet, glistening light.
> Dear mother, the window is dark again,
> But you are in the light because
> I finished all that consequence.*

But, after the death of the boy, there yet remains the consequence of the crime 'upon themselves'. This is also a ground of the remorse that the spirit suffers. The crime that the woman committed upon herself was the fouling of her own nature by lust, as the old man explains in the central speech of the play when he imagines the bridal night:

> She has gone down to open the door.
> This night she is no better than her man
> And does not mind that he is half drunk,
> She is mad about him. They mount the stairs,
> She brings him into her own chamber . . .

This, and the meditation that follows, is an extremely crucial part of the play, to which I shall return. For the moment, it must be clear to the audience that into *this* re-enactment no action of the old man, of the living 'others', can possibly enter in order to cut its knot. The point is stressed by the old man's ineffectual cry 'Do not let him touch you! . . . Deaf! Both deaf!' The woman cannot

---

* The tree is a family-'tree' and also stands for the condition of the shade's soul. Fifty years ago it had 'Green leaves, ripe leaves, leaves thick as butter, Fat greasy life'. Then it was blasted and became the bare tree of the play, which resembles the image of the tree seen in the bitter glass held up by demons before the woman who barters her beauty in 'The Two Trees'. Through its branches fly the 'ravens of unresting thought':

> For there a fatal image grows
> That the stormy night receives,
> Roots half-hidden under snows,
> Broken boughs and blackened leaves.
> For all things turn to barrenness
> In the dim glass the demons hold.
>   (Variorum edition of the *Poems*, p. 135)

106

be freed from that aspect of her crime which is equivalent to her self-degradation. For this act, even after death, brings with it pleasure as well as remorse, as the old man suggests. The remorseful spirit must, in order to be free of it, repeat, explore, or dream through the crime which it committed during life; but in this case the renewal of the act, because of the nature of the act, renews the self-degrading pleasure that accompanied it. Thus the very consequence from which release is sought—self-degradation—is entailed upon the mother's spirit each time she lives through her transgression. It is as pretty an entanglement as Yeats ever devised. There is none like it in *A Vision*, perhaps because he had not yet seen, when he wrote that work, into what complexities his notion of the dead who are obliged to live through their transgressions might be developed if only the transgressions were complicated enough. The case is one, as the old man at length perceives, which only the 'mercy of God' can solve. Hence his final prayer. Yeats— can it be said?—has at last found a use for God. He is called in because the Yeatsian dead can no longer manage by themselves, so extraordinary has their private purgatory become. There is no God amongst the discarnate spirits of *A Vision*.

The subject of *Purgatory* is an extension of one that had been touched upon in *The Dreaming of the Bones*. Both plays are concerned with the remorse of the dead, and in the earlier one there is a hint that the living, the 'others' who suffer the consequences of the crimes of the dead, may help them. In *The Dreaming of the Bones* the soldier's forgiveness might have assuaged the torment of Dermot and Dervorgilla. The whole subject of *Purgatory* is such an assuagement, which is indeed accomplished, although under the conditions making for final frustration that have just been examined. That in this play the act of intervention is a murder, not pardon, is necessitated by the story chosen. It affords a measure of the difference between the finished, melancholy and somewhat self-conscious beauty of *The Dreaming of the Bones* and the squalor, sexuality and violence of *Purgatory*.

The development on this scale of a theme which *The Dreaming of the Bones* merely sketches meant that Yeats had to find a fresh dramatic form. The making of a self-subsistent image of phantasmic suffering such as he gives us in *The Dreaming of the Bones* and at the centre of *The Words upon the Window-pane* can no longer be his aim. His subject, which is now chiefly about an attempt at intervention by the living in the life of the dead, requires that he concern himself with the living, with the unfinished life, not with the intense rendering of an unearthly suffering. The story told in *Purgatory* is one that leaves on the ears of the audience a cry reaching outside the play to God, unlike the final words of both *The Dreaming of the Bones* and *The Words upon the Window-pane*, which fold the plays back upon themselves so that they contemplate their own stories. *Purgatory* is an image deliberately left incomplete, a human image, rather than one that shows the dead trapped in the vortex of their own suffering. Compared with the earlier plays, it is, as it were, slewed round; ghosts and men have exchanged positions. In *Purgatory* the man is what we see first, and beyond and through him the voiceless shades pose in a window like lantern-slides upon which he discourses. This is very different from *The Dreaming of the Bones*, where Dermot and Dervorgilla dominate a human being whose representative status matters more than his individuality, and from *The Words upon the Window-pane*, where Mrs. Henderson, asleep in her chair, mediates to us the full force of the passionate shade. In *Purgatory* we are deeply engaged with the old man.

One of his functions is to tell us what the apparitions mean and to what realm they belong. He thus performs the task allotted to Dr. Trench in *The Words upon the Window-pane* and to the conversation between the soldier and the lovers about the different kinds of hauntings in the first portion of *The Dreaming of the Bones*. His speech, therefore, part of which I have quoted on page 105, explains all that the spectator needs to know about the condition of the dead in the play. But it could not have been spoken by an entirely naturalistic character. If the old man really 'knew' all that, he would not have acted as he does, or at least would not have been surprised that his action was ultimately without effect in releasing his mother's shade from its dream. This is one of those carelessnesses about orthodox realism that also occur in *The Death of Cuchulain* and convey, however mysteriously, a sense of theatrical power. This does not mean that the old man and his whole situation are not sharply individualized with the aid of as much graphic detail as the miniature size of the play permits. His description of the groom's murder,[44] for example, carries conviction:

just so might the brutal country tragedy have happened. When
the old man speaks of it, possessed though his mind is with heredity and phantoms, he looks round to make sure that no one can
overhear, and similarly, when he kills the boy, he makes certain
that nobody, except the phantom groom, is watching.

There are things, then, which the old man both 'knows' and
does not *know*, and what he does not *know*, or does not fully
understand, is an important element in his tragedy. He has learning, which he obtained in spite of his polluted origin, and he
cherishes the things of learning and ancestral beauty. He speaks
of the 'great people' of the old estate, their love of the demesne
and the flowering trees that were cut down by the degenerate
inheritor, and of his own education:

> some
> Half-loved me for my half of her:
> A gamekeeper's wife taught me to read,
> A Catholic curate taught me Latin.
> There were old books and books made fine
> By eighteenth-century French binding, books
> Modern and ancient, books by the ton.

But at a crucial moment this sort of learning becomes a crazy
parody of itself. In the long central speech, during which the consummation of the fatal marriage is re-enacted, the old man tells
the audience enough for them to understand the nature of the
mother's self-degradation, the consequence that she commits upon
herself; but he does not understand it himself.

> she must live
> Through everything in exact detail,
> Driven to it by remorse, and yet
> Can she renew the sexual act
> And find no pleasure in it, and if not,
> If pleasure and remorse must both be there,
> Which is the greater?
> I lack schooling.
> Go fetch Tertullian; he and I
> Will ravel all that problem out
> Whilst those two lie upon the mattress
> Begetting me.

The call for Tertullian is a kind of witless joke on his part. F. A. C. Wilson's straight-faced comment that he 'refers to Tertullian's treatise on the mixed nature of the soul, *de Anima*' [45] seems to me to miss the point. The point is that the old man is unable to relate what is happening with what as a character inside the play's action he does not *know*, namely, that the dead

> know at last
> The consequence of those transgressions
> Whether upon others or upon themselves . . .
> upon themselves,
> There is no help but in themselves
> And in the mercy of God.

If he were able to collate his two kinds of knowledge, which being in a state of crazy half-knowledge, he is not, he would know his mother's condition to its depths; he would not suppose that the killing of the boy could do more than momentarily assuage her torment. This state of half-knowledge is his hereditary condition entailed upon him by his polluted blood. It is his tragic fate. It is that which engineers the catastrophe, just as Cuchulain's movement of courage in *At the Hawk's Well* frustrates itself because of his fate. The old man, the son of a groom, conceived in drunkenness, cannot be a sage, although there are moments when he pathetically tries to behave like one.

All the old man's qualities are quartered with his vices in this way. He acts to save his mother, but has brutalized his son, and given him, as he tells him:

> the education that befits
> A bastard that a pedlar got
> Upon a tinker's daughter in a ditch.

He is capable of vision, but breaks away from it to struggle with the boy for the bag of money. His past is like this, too: the gently-nurtured boy who killed his father and hid the body in the burning house. That he can say that he is 'a wretched foul old man' is his noble trait, because it expresses his awareness of degradation, which is not present in the boy his son yet further degenerated from the stock; but it is also the truth.

The central figure is thus hereditarily endowed with worth and vileness, and these are interlocked in his nature as Othello's nobility is interlocked with his crime or Coriolanus's manhood with his childishness. I think that we are meant to be aware of this when we contemplate his final acts. He kills the boy in order to break the links of consequence, but the act itself partakes of his double nature. It is done by all that is good in him, but it is done in the condition of half-knowledge necessitated by what he is, and it is also a horrible crime. This last is true if I am right in thinking that the dramatist did not mean us to regard it in a coldly theoretical way simply as something done by the living for the sake of the dead and therefore justifiable even if largely ineffectual. The image of the father killing his son duplicates too dreadfully the earlier image of the son killing the father; the knife with which it is done is the same knife, the vile knife which 'cuts my dinner', like the Blind Man's knife in *The Death of Cuchulain*; the hand which drives it is the same hand:

> My father and my son on the same jack-knife!

'He stabs again and again', says the stage-direction. The act is a crime because it explicitly shares features with the parricide which, when he was sixteen, was the old man's first manifestation in action of his tainted stock. The nursery-rhyme which he chants as he murders the boy adds a special ghastliness. The sacrifice turns out to be murder after all.

There is great irony in it, too. For this act, which is designed to finish 'all that consequence', and indeed does so, is also a fresh addition to the links of consequence. Instead of a lengthening chain, it makes of them a circular band of horror, a wheel of fire: the son kills the father, the father kills the son. And all this has failed to break the suffering spirit's bondage. Thus the old man, as this realization breaks upon him and he turns away from his acts to pray, does rightly in that he prays for the living as well as for the dead:

> O God,
> Release my mother's soul from its dream!
> Mankind can do no more. Appease
> The misery of the living and the remorse of the dead.

Purgatory is the most successful of Yeats's three attempts to dramatize one stage of the progress of the soul from grave to cradle, or from grave to beatitude. He chose the only one of the visionary phases which could be adapted for human theatrical life. The imagination that conceived the 'dreaming back' had that much in common with the dramatic imagination. The purgatorial state was made to fit forms so different from one another as the Noh, the naturalistic play in prose, and a Shakespearian tragedy in miniature.

There is room for another comment on the relation between playwright and philosopher. In *The Words upon the Window-pane* Yeats has suspended his own convictions for the play's sake, and we are invited to put our own interpretation on what we have seen. But the convictions remain there rigidly in the centre of the play in the image of Swift's ghost and its suffering and re-enactment. This makes the rest of the play seem merely the scaffolding for the central event, the mystery. The human observers are grouped in a circle round the appalling, unreachable voice; the construction of the play mirrors the arrangements for a séance, or a revelation. As in *The Resurrection*, Yeats has turned the tables upon the naturalistic drama by exploding it from inside; from its shattered ruins there arises the terrible image of an utterly different kind of life. But in *Purgatory* the convictions are dissolved into the life of the protagonist; our attention is fixed upon the old man's story and his divided nature. The dead of *A Vision* and of the other plays live, although their condition is vividly enough rendered, a schematic life, each in the appropriate circle of their purgatory; but in the last play the old man's attempt to break into the circle, driven by furious pity and by jealous hatred of his own evil as embodied in his son, is his own story and no ghost shares it.

Chapter Six

For Reason, Miracle

All things have value according to the clarity of their expression of themselves.

I

THE two plays about Christianity, *Calvary* (1921) and *The Resurrection* (begun in 1925 and later rewritten), are often coupled together, and have been used mainly, if not entirely, as clues to Yeats's philosophy of history, his theism, or atheism.[1]

On Christianity, so far as they are relevant to the plays, his thoughts can be described briefly, without doing them very much injustice. He saw the pagan world, in particular the world of Greece and Rome, as a *primary* civilization; at the time of Christ's coming it was drawing to its foreordained end in the cyclical movement of history and was becoming subject to the loss of control which heralded the birth of the next age. This next, or Christian, age was *antithetical* to its predecessor. It begins with the Annunciation of a God who seeks to live like a man while teaching that man must seek to live like God. Yeats's favourite gnomic phrase for this, which he uses at the end of *The Resurrection* and elsewhere, was a saying borrowed from Heraclitus: 'God and man die each other's life, live each other's death.' This riddling aphorism, which can be shown to have a connexion with the lines in 'Byzantium'

> I hail the superhuman,
> I call it death-in-life and life-in-death,

can be sorted out, and the chief *loci* indicated, in this way:

(1) God dies man's life, or life-in-death: the dead God is like a live man (the resurrection, the journey to Emmaus, the beating heart of the resurrected Christ in *The Resurrection*).

(2) God lives man's death, or death-in-life: the eternal God becomes a man, and dies.

(3) Man dies God's life, or life-in-death: the dead man is like a living God; he cannot die, or cannot find the death appropriate to man (Lazarus in *Calvary*).

(4) Man lives God's death, or death-in-life: the living man endeavours to live like an immortal, spiritual creature, to 'ascend to Heaven', or to be, like the resurrected Christ, 'a phantom with a beating heart'. In this way man diminishes his humanity, and the self no longer claims

> as by a soldier's right
> A charter to commit the crime once more.[2]

Man renounces the self and tries to live according to a pattern drawn from the God who dies. The saint and the anchorite who retire to the desert and whose 'joy is to be nothing, to do nothing, to think nothing' [3] become the supreme models for humanity:

> Fix every wandering thought upon
> That quarter where all thought is done.[4]

They become vessels filled with the divine life, not their own life; their desert-world is 'changed into featureless clay and can be run through the fingers'.[5]

The Resurrection, in particular, if suitably correlated with other documents, can be made to yield much complicated information about such matters as the historical cycles, Yeats's views on Babylonian astronomy, or his knowledge of what a certain fourth-century sophist, whose words are recorded in Eunapius's life of Aedesius, said about 'a fabulous formless darkness tyrannizing over the fairest things on earth'.[6]

Calvary and *The Resurrection* are partial and dramatic actualizations of this complex of ideas, especially as it bears upon the role of Jesus the Man-God. But they are not 'texts for exposition', and there is some danger that their properties as plays may go unexamined.

A writer of drama must observe the form as carefully as if it were a sonnet, but he must always deny that there is any subject-matter which is in itself dramatic—any especial round of emotion fitted to the stage, or that a play has no need to await its audience or to create the interest it lives by.[7]

It would, of course, be pointless to deny that these are plays of ideas, and that the first impulse that the student of Yeats's work as a whole is likely to feel when he encounters them will be one of curiosity about Yeats's readings of religion and history. If this were all, they could, by such tests as the poet himself was normally willing to apply, be written off as dramatic failures. But the fact that they are plays of ideas (a respectable enough theatrical kind) has its own aspect of formal significance. Do they create the interest they live by?

II

Little attention has ever been paid to *Calvary*. Sturge Moore, when he was designing the cover for *Four Plays for Dancers*, liked it least of the four.[8] It is certainly in a different category from the other plays in that collection. In it, Christ 'dreams His passion through' and is confronted with images of those whom he cannot save: Lazarus, Judas, the Three Roman Soldiers, who ask nothing of God, and Heron, Eagle, and Swan, which are content in their solitude. With its Musicians' songs and descriptions of the scene, its bare stage, masked actors, and final dance (of the Roman soldiers round the Cross), the play has the familiar Noh features. It also has the iterative image-cluster—this time of bird and animal—which Yeats believed to be a principal device of the Noh. In a play on so tiny a scale everything counts, and this imagery contributes much to its structure.

The first song for the folding and unfolding of the cloth about the heron staring at its own image in the moonlit water, with its refrain 'God has not died for the white heron', is not the key to the meaning of the play. It is the first of four variations on the theme of Christ's powerlessness to save those who can live without salvation. The play consists of these four variations; the theme itself is not heard except through them. It is important, if obscurity is to be avoided, that the playwright should show us how each variation relates to the common theme. The refrain of the song about the heron is clear enough; it is more doubtful if the full thematic significance of the rest of it can be grasped at a first hearing, although the notion of crazy self-absorption is plainly put:

> Although half famished he'll not dare
> Dip or do anything but stare
> Upon the glittering image of a heron,
> That now is lost and now is there.[9] *

The songs in *Calvary* have other functions to perform in addition to constituting the first variation on the common theme. It follows that they relate to that theme differently from the way in which the three self-contained episodes of Lazarus, Judas, and the Roman Soldiers relate to it. Their chill detachment expresses the 'subjectivity' of a world detached from Christ; it also holds the play within a frame and helps to give it the quality of 'distance' which Yeats admired in the Noh plays.[10] By establishing its bounds so clearly the songs order the life of the play, and maintain this control by means of the image of the heron, which recurs in

---

* No music for the songs in *Calvary* is printed in *Four Plays for Dancers*. Yeats had once believed in the possibility of establishing a right relationship between words and music in his plays:

If a song is brought into a play it does not matter to what school the musician belongs if every word, if every cadence, is audible and expressive as if it were spoken . . . One must ask . . . for music that shall mean nothing, or next to nothing, apart from the words (*Plays and Controversies*, pp. 129–30).

But he despaired of finding an adequately submissive musician, and had by now, as he put it in his 'Commentary' on *The King of the Great Clock Tower* (Dublin, Cuala Press, 1934, p. 18), 'given up the fight', and cynically resigned himself to the fact that no audience would ever be able to hear properly any words of his which were accompanied by music. His cynicism took the form of regarding his songs as 'secrets'—always in the sense that he did not expect the words to be heard in the theatre (but they could be consulted in the book), and sometimes also in the sense that the song was *about* a mystery or secret. This hidden meaning could also be solved by 'turning to a note' (see *Four Plays for Dancers*, p. 135; the Cuala Press edition of *The King of the Great Clock Tower*, p. 19). The degree of 'secrecy' in the meaning of the songs seems to vary from play to play, but they are not often as obscure as they are in *The Resurrection*, where the songs have a special history (see below p. 127). For the songs in *The King of the Great Clock Tower* and *A Full Moon in March*, see below, p. 162.

the body of the work. Such strict ordering is the more needed here because the play has no single central action, as *The Dreaming of the Bones* has, nor structural core, as *The Words upon the Window-pane* and *Purgatory* have. It simply presents us with a series of events; each of these are of the same length and importance, and there is no 'working to a climax'.[11] The danger that the series will break down into arbitrary and inconsequential incidents is avoided by what the songs do.

There is a contrast, not of theme, but of style and feeling, between the songs and the other elements in the play. These other elements are centred on the rendering of Lazarus, Judas, and the Soldiers. The songs are impersonal, remote, and symbolic; Lazarus and the others are individually, almost naturalistically, done. So, too, is the Musicians' description of the scene when it is compared with their opening song. A similar contrast is observable between Christ and the other characters.

It is important to understand that the play does not attempt to actualize Christ's suffering. The play is his 'dreaming-back':

> Good Friday's come,
> The day whereon Christ dreams His passion through.
> He climbs up hither but as a dreamer climbs.
> The cross that but exists because He dreams it
> Shortens His breath and wears away His strength.

This theme is not used in the way it is used in the plays discussed in the preceding chapter, but in order to make the suffering remote rather than actual. Christ's speeches are all very short (the longest is of four lines) and they often take the form of oracular utterances, majestic and theophanic: 'I have conquered death And all the dead shall be raised up again'; 'I do my Father's will'; 'My Father put all men into my hands'. Christ is at the centre of the scene not as a tortured victim but as the pantokrator, Byzantine and unrealistic, rigid like the figure in an icon. There is only one place where he betrays this role: in the Musician's description of the three Marys casting their tears upon the ground before his blood-dabbled feet.[12]

By contrast, Lazarus and Judas are both individualized. The part of each builds up towards a longer speech in which this individuality and realism come to a climax. Lazarus reproaches Christ for dragging him up to the light, demands Christ's death in exchange for the one he has been robbed of, and describes (with one of the animal-images that run through the play) how the theft was accomplished:

> Alive I never could escape your love,
> And when I sickened towards my death I thought
> I'll to the desert, or chuckle in a corner
> Mere ghost, a solitary thing. I died
> And saw no more until I saw you stand
> In the opening of the tomb; 'Come out!' you called;
> You dragged me to the light as boys drag out
> A rabbit when they have dug its hole away;
> And now with all the shouting at your heels
> You travel towards the death I am denied.

Lazarus, unlike Christ, is visualized; his face is death-hungry, and the crowd shrinks from him. He beats in vain against the marmoreal stillness of the central figure.

So also with Judas. Lazarus is an emotional figure, thirsting after the personal death beyond his reach. Judas is intellectual; his business is to conduct a theological dispute with Christ during which he says fifty words to every two or three of the other speaker. He betrayed Christ in order to be free of him, in order to be himself again and not an object of the all-powerful God. Christ's statement that God had determined from the beginning that somebody should betray him produces Judas's long assertion of identity, corresponding to Lazarus's speech:

> It was decreed that somebody betray you—
> I'd thought of that—but not that I should do it,
> I the man Judas, born on such a day,
> In such a village, such and such his parents;
> Nor that I'd go with my old coat upon me
> To the High Priest, and chuckle to myself
> As people chuckle when alone, and that I'd do it
> For thirty pieces and no more, no less,
> And neither with a nod, a look, nor a sent message,
> But with a kiss upon your cheek. I did it,
> I, Judas, and no other man, and now
> You cannot even save me.

Browning might have written in this fashion had he attempted a dramatic monologue for Judas. But all this intellectual energy is at a discount. Christ keeps his marble repose. During the final episode of the Roman Soldiers he speaks only two lines. The Soldiers are those who cast all upon the throw of the dice, asking nothing of Providence because they are content with Fortune. Their dance before the motionless figure on the cross repeats the contrast between stillness and movement.

These contrasts between the active and fixed, personal and impersonal, suffering which reaches out in gloating and accusation and suffering which is withdrawn and symbolic, are the formal devices fundamental to the play. They are also, of course, its larger meaning. The forms have been used to convey the ideas in this play of ideas. These are individuals who reject Christ because they cling to their selfhood, personal death, and freedom from the invading God who wants to turn them into what he is; they are 'subjective' men in the special Yeatsian sense.

The construction, both formal and conceptual, is completed by what we discover about Christ. Just as Lazarus, Judas, and the Soldiers form one movement, so Christ and the birds of the Musicians' songs form the counter-movement. The birds are the completest symbols of self-sufficient isolation:

> The geer-eagle has chosen his part
> In blue deep of the upper air
> Where one-eyed day can meet his stare;
> He is content with his savage heart.

> God has not appeared to the birds.

God has not appeared to them, but this God is like them. By this subtle collocation (the songs are finally seen to be *about* Christ as well as about the birds), Yeats makes his last points. The stillness and loneliness of Christ are enhanced, and the songs are tied into the main antithesis of the play. As Yeats would have put it when writing in another mode, it is the subjective God who calls upon men to be his objects, who pours his own spirit into them. During a phase of civilization such as the Greek and Roman was, men are permitted to be their own objects: 'Man . . . remains separate. He does not surrender his soul. He keeps his privacy' (The Goddess, in Yeats's favourite Homeric image, takes Achilles by his yellow hair, not by his soul). During the Christian era, God, unique and solitary as the Eagle, which is the King of Birds, seeks, like the heron in the stream, to find everywhere his own image and to change what he loves into himself, unlike the lovers in *A Vision* who 'would not change that which we love'. When God acts towards men he acts towards his own image in them. Thus, 'the Good Samaritan discovers himself in the likeness of another, covered with sores and abandoned by thieves . . . and in that other serves himself'.[13] God pities men to the degree that they are not like him and must, for example, die; so he raises Lazarus. His power is absolute, so he can make Judas into his instrument. In *Calvary* both Judas and Lazarus are conceived as relicts of the elder civilization; they do not want to be completely God's objects but to remain themselves; they want to keep their subjectivity and selfhood, their privacy, and are not willing to 'sacrifice everything that the divine suffering might . . . descend into one's mind and soul' and to allow 'God . . . to take complete possession'.[14] The playwright's mind, as well as his eye, has seen Christ as the pantokrator in the Byzantine dome looking everywhere and asking for everything.

III

Calvary is successful in giving the 'feel' of the ideas upon which it is a play, although these are not given in the terminology of the metaphysical treatise. They are presented as movement round a medial stillness, as vortices of the intellectually active, death-hungry, or dancing selfhoods arranged about the god. The play does not quicken or deepen as it grows; it shows what it is by standing still and is short enough for the audience to hold it in its mind as a whole and range back and forth over it as they speculate on its meaning. This is an unusual form for a play of ideas, where normally we expect the ideas to be developed dialectically. In *The Resurrection* there is much more development of the dialectical variety. Some of the ideas are directly expressed in debates between the characters; the characters themselves are representative men, explaining what they represent instead of, as in *Calvary*, leaving it to be deduced from the way they describe what they have done. *The Resurrection* is more, however, than merely a discussion-play. Events are shown, not just talked about. And all the explanatory talk and commentary are in the end subordinated to the showing forth of their own meaning which is done by the events themselves. These events are arranged in a more ordinary dramatic pattern than the one to be found in *Calvary*. It is not a static pattern, ordered by interlocking contrasts, but a sequential one of exposition, conflict leading to mounting tension, and exploding into a catastrophe.

Yeats worked hard to achieve just this. In 1925, we are told, a first sketch of the play was read out 'to a few people, a Cabinet minister among them, who were frigid'.[15] This was the 'chaotic dialogue' of which he wrote in a letter to Mrs. Shakespear in December, 1930: 'But now I have dramatic tension throughout.'[16] The narrative design and many of the ideas are curiously adumbrated in a passage written nearly thirty years before (in 1904). Its imagery suggests the Christian referents at the back of the writer's mind:

A Civilisation is very like a man or a woman, for it comes in but a few years into its beauty, and its strength, and then, while many years go by, it gathers and makes order about it, the strength and beauty going out of it the while, until in the end it lies there with its limbs straightened out and a clean linen cloth folded upon it. That may well be, and yet we need not follow among the mourners, for it may be, before they are at the tomb, a messenger will run out of the hills and touch the pale lips with a red ember, and wake the limbs to the disorder and the tumult that is life. Though he does not come, even so we will keep from among the mourners and hold some cheerful conversation among ourselves; for has not Virgil, a knowledgeable man and a wizard, foretold that other Argonauts shall row between cliff and cliff, and other fair-haired Achæans sack another Troy?[17]

The notion of holding 'some cheerful conversation' while an era lies dead seems a little touch of Lewis Carroll in the night of Yeats's later imagination of disaster as famously expressed in 'The Second Coming'. But in *The Resurrection* the allusions to the messenger, the mourners, and the Virgilian prophecy are made actual.

The play begins in a bustle of apparently unrelated movements; it is only gradually that we learn the rationale that makes a single event of them. The eleven apostles, unseen by the audience, are gathered in the upper room after the crucifixion. The mob is 'busy hunting Christians', but three followers of Jesus, a Hebrew, a Greek, and a Syrian (absent from the stage when the play begins) are ready to defend the stairway with their lives. Meanwhile another mob, the followers of Dionysus, are out in the streets dancing and worshipping as they carry the image of their dead god.

There is further movement in the argument between Greek and Hebrew. Both are subjective men, like Lazarus and Judas in *Calvary*. To the Greek, Jesus was not a man but a spirit:

We Greeks understand these things. No god has ever been buried; no god has ever suffered. Christ only seemed to be born, only seemed to eat, seemed to sleep, seemed to walk, seemed to die.[18]

The gods do not covet earthly bodies, but are discovered only through contemplation; God does not 'die man's life'. The Hebrew is shocked because the Greek thinks of Jesus's life as only a simulacrum of human life, and of the crucifixion as a shadow-play. To the Hebrew, it was the suffering of a man, 'the best man who ever lived', who 'some day when he was very tired . . . thought that he himself was the Messiah'. In his way, the Hebrew is glad that this has now been proved to be the case by the defeat and death of the supposed Messiah; earlier, when he acknowledged the Messianic claim, he had anticipated with dread the terrible burden this was going to impose on him, robbing him of his subjectivity and making him simply an object of the immanent God:

One had to give up all worldly knowledge, all ambition, do nothing of one's own will. Only the divine could have any reality. God had to take complete possession. It must be a terrible thing when one is old, and the tomb round the corner, to think of all the ambitions one has put aside; to think, perhaps, a great deal about women. I want to marry and have children.

He no longer has to become an anchorite and retire to the featureless desert.

If this were all, we would have the ideas clearly expressed but not dramatically presented. But Yeats relates this ideological argument between Greek and Hebrew both to the events of the plot and to a meaningful thematic accompaniment. Out of these three elements he contrives a dramatic unity. Thus the Hebrew is made to state the Christian position from the point of view of a believer in it who has just received proof of its falsity; he has reverted to what he was before the failed Messiah came. The Greek, meanwhile, is waiting for the proof of *his* position:

THE HEBREW

Proof?

THE GREEK

I shall have proof before nightfall.

THE HEBREW

You talk wildly, but a masterless dog can bay the moon.

The Greek has sent the third man, the Syrian, to the tomb 'to prove that there is nothing there', and he expects the messenger to return with the certain news that 'Jesus never had a human body',

that he is a phantom and can pass through that wall; that he will so pass; that he will pass through this room; that he himself will speak to the apostles

It is his confidence in this that prepares for the moment of intense excitement at the end of the play. Thus the Hebrew, with his 'proof' drawn from the crucifixion, and the Greek, with his 'proof' drawn from the resurrection, are not merely debating incompatible points of view; in judging by events, they relate their argument to a narrative sequence; the events in their turn share in the debate because they are assimilated into it as proofs. Sequence and debate are both put into time and await resolution by it.

The debate is joined to the accompaniment of a background of 'irrational force' and 'animal chaos'—the phrases are used in *A Vision*—which is represented by the worshippers of Dionysus in the street below. Their rattles, drums, and cries, and their song ('Astraea's holy child') sound at intervals throughout the play. The worshippers abandon themselves to their god and become completely his objects; 'three days after the full moon, a full moon in March, they sing the death of the god and pray for his resurrection'. Although the parallels do not escape the audience, the Greek

123

and the Hebrew are quite unaware of them. The self-abandon-
ment, the monstrous ceremonies, the boys from the theatre
dressed as girls, the barbaric din are merely disgusting, the work
of mad, ambiguous creatures, 'such a thing [as] had never happened in this city before'. In providing an accompaniment of this
kind Yeats was doing more than supplying factitious excitement
or indulging himself in an exercise in comparative religion. There
are, of course, good reasons in *A Vision* for the presence of such
sectaries at such a moment in time,* but they are not given in
the play. What the audience is given, in place of this kind of
detail, is the juxtaposition of two characters to whom religion is
a matter for individual response, definition, discussion, and proof,
with the worshippers of the dismembered god, to whom it is a
matter for collective howling, drumming, and orgiastic frenzy.
This is a contrast, achieved by formal antitheses (speech and song,
beaten drums and anxious talk), which is similar in kind to those
in *Calvary* between one mode of being and another. It generates
the sense that the world of *The Resurrection* is throbbing with
forces that make the stance, even the intellectuality (their power
to argue about the issues), of Greek and Hebrew things which
belong to a habit that is threatened and about to pass away.

But in *The Resurrection*, as not in *Calvary*, the spectator is made
to participate by having the argument demonstrated upon his
own pulse. The Greek awaiting his proof and the issue that hangs
in the air between the reasoners and the worshippers, the frenetic
sect and the ordered cities, cohere together as they move together
into a final event of compelling theatrical authority, the most con-
summate moment of its kind in all Yeats's plays. The Syrian messenger returns; Yeats must have been sorry that he could not call
him a Babylonian, but he got as near to this as he could. 'Like a
drunken man' he announces the tale told him by the Galilaean
women, of the appearance of Jesus to them, and of the empty
sepulchre. He is convinced that something has happened which is

* Yeats believed that the Second Annunciation (the first was that to Leda)
was preceded by obscure intimations in the form of the oriental cults of the
Roman empire which were influenced by Babylonian astrology and astronomy.
These were the 'peacock's cry', the final loss of control of the old primary
civilization as it was transformed into the antithetical Christian era (see *A
Vision* [1937], p. 268).

outside the kind of knowledge and order to which the other two men are clinging. His excitement, contributing a note of hysteria to the argument, makes it intenser in tone and more rapid in pace, for the Greek and Hebrew had been doing their duty as defenders of the apostles in a spirit of last-ditch, disciplined Stoicism:

THE SYRIAN

... What if at the moment when knowledge and order seem complete that something appears? [*He has begun to laugh.*]

THE HEBREW

Stop laughing.

THE SYRIAN

What if the irrational return? What if the circle begin again?

THE HEBREW

Stop! He laughed when he saw Calvary through the window, and now you laugh.

THE GREEK

He too has lost control of himself.

THE HEBREW

Stop, I tell you. [*Drums and rattles.*]

THE SYRIAN

But I am not laughing. It is the people out there who are laughing.

THE HEBREW

No, they are shaking rattles and beating drums.

The Greek's laughter was close to the philosopher's cackle at a well-conducted argument; the Syrian's to the hysteria of the worshippers' self-abandon, merging into the noise in the streets.

Both Greek and Hebrew refuse to accept the implications of his message. To the Hebrew, it is the wishful 'dreams of women'; to the Greek, it is his proof at last, that Jesus was a phantom, whose reappearance will show that God does not overwhelm man with miracle but permits him to keep his privacy. Meanwhile, the Dionysans, who have gone away to bury their god, are returning through the streets with their cry of 'God has arisen'.

Their dance is suspended suddenly as they turn eyes blind with ecstasy towards the house; two religions melt into one as the converging lines of the drama touch and what was an analogue becomes the thing itself. The dramatic climax shows Yeats combining his long-held idea that men seek reality with the slow toil of their weakness and are smitten from the boundless and unforeseen with a technique learnt from the Japanese Noh; for, as Earl Miner has observed, 'the climax occurs at the point where the supernatural being (Christ) reveals his true form and brings, as in nō, spiritual enlightenment'.[19] Even after the figure of Christ has made its silent entry, the empirical Greek is determined that what his senses will tell him will be the truth that he expects:

There is nothing here but a phantom, it has no flesh and blood. Because I know the truth I am not afraid. Look, I will touch it. It may be hard under my hand like a statue—I have heard of such things—or my hand may pass through it—but there is no flesh and blood. [*He goes slowly up to the figure and passes his hand over its side.*] The heart of a phantom is beating! The heart of a phantom is beating! [*He screams. The figure of Christ crosses the stage and passes into the inner room.*]

It is one of the oddest critical misjudgements that a dramatist who can contrive a moment so supremely thrilling as this—one in which all the movements of the play blaze up together into meaning and theatrical effect—should have been accused of writing plays which 'are little more than charades'.[20] 'I felt', Yeats wrote, recording how he encountered the original of the incident in Sir William Crookes's *Studies in Psychical Research*, '. . . the terror of the supernatural described by Job.'[21] He successfully administers to his audience the 'violent shock' which induces a sense of spiritual reality.[22] The 'terror of the supernatural', which Miss Mackenna merely talked about in *The Words upon the Window-pane* passes before the face: 'Belief comes from shock and is not desired.'[23]

As plays of ideas, *Calvary* and *The Resurrection* are different in method, although they use a roughly similar set of ideas. *Calvary* presents its audience with an image for it to contemplate and does not attempt to draw its hearers into it more than is needed to get them to pay attention. *The Resurrection* is more dynamic; by increasingly converging lines of movement Yeats brings the spectator into position so that he can administer his 'violent shock'. Each play follows its chosen form 'as carefully as if it were a sonnet'. Yeats was willing to experiment, especially after he had discovered the Noh and completed *At the Hawk's Well* in 1916. The Noble Plays themselves were after all, he said, something that 'need absorb no one's life'. When he had done enough in that kind he would 'record all discoveries of method and turn to something else'.* 24

* I have not discussed the two songs with which *The Resurrection* opens and closes. Famous as poems from their inclusion in *The Tower* (1928), they were an addition to the original scheme of the play (see *Wheels and Butterflies*, p. 111); the last of the four stanzas was a still later addition, post-dating *The Tower*. Although, except for this stanza, they are lyrical meditations on the theme of the play, intelligible in the light of it, they seem completely detachable from it, unlike the songs in *Calvary*.

Chapter Seven

The Beasts

---

hoping to find once more,
Being by Calvary's turbulence unsatisfied,
The uncontrollable mystery on the bestial floor.

I

'FOR years', Yeats wrote in the Introduction to *The Resurrection*, 'I have been preoccupied with a certain myth that was in itself a reply to a myth' and went on to say:

I do not mean a fiction, but one of those statements our nature is compelled to make and employ as a truth though there cannot be sufficient evidence. When I was a boy everybody talked about progress, and rebellion against my elders took the form of aversion to that myth. I took satisfaction in certain public disasters, felt a sort of ecstasy in the contemplation of ruin.[1]

The sense that the world was awaiting a revelation that would destroy old things and bring a different order to birth was one that persecuted him as much as it inspired him. It grew slowly more elaborate, aided and transformed by the discovery of images. Destruction acquired its complement: the generation, out of a violent reversal of the old order, of a new time.

The poets, rebels, and outcasts, who are the central figures in the early stories in *The Secret Rose* and *The Tables of the Law* (1897), are impelled to reject the life around them and travel the 'roads of the world', searching, like the old man in 'The Heart of

Spring' for something they cannot define, 'the secret of life', the 'Great Secret'.[2] They choose 'that beauty which seems unearthly',[3] and discover that there is something in their natures which cannot be content with ordinary loves—one of the themes of 'The Wisdom of the King', where the monarch who has been gifted with the feathers of the magical hawk instead of hair strides from his palace into the unknown world and is never seen again. Red Hanrahan is a wanderer and outcast of this kind; persecuted and inspired, he is a victim as well as a teacher and poet. His visions are of the Sidhe, Cathleen ni Houlihan, and a Celtic Valhalla whose music is 'the continual clashing of swords'.[4]

Lady Gregory had helped to purge the Red Hanrahan stories of some of their excessive ornament and to make his story part of a familiar Irish landscape, and it is the tales about Owen Aherne and Michael Robartes that bring us closest to Yeats himself at this time. They are filled with confusion, argument, and colour—faked patrology, alchemical rites, sacred books with jewelled covers that enshrine Byzantine paintings. The character of Aherne expresses most completely the 'consuming thirst for destruction' which also entails the destruction of the self:

More orthodox in most of his beliefs than Michael Robartes, he had surpassed him in a fanciful hatred of all life, and this hatred had found expression in the curious paradox—half borrowed from some fanatical monk, half invented by himself—that the beautiful arts were sent into the world to overthrow nations, and finally life herself, by sowing everywhere unlimited desires, like torches thrown into a burning city.[5]

The world and the future that Robartes and Aherne seek are never very clearly seen. The stories dramatize the seeking rather than the finding: 'I know nothing certain as yet but this', Aherne cries, 'I am to become completely alive, that is, completely passionate, for beauty is only another name for perfect passion':

I shall create a world where the whole lives of men shall be articulated and simplified as if seventy years were but one moment, or as they were the leaping of a fish or the opening of a flower.[6]

And the search is attended by nightmare terrors, visions of evil as well as of supernatural good, like the great worm which seems to clutch Aherne in its folds, as it had clutched Red Hanrahan in another story.[7] The narrator fights against being swept away 'into an indefinite world which fills me with terror':

a man is a great man just in so far as he can make his mind reflect everything with indifferent precision like a mirror. . . . I command you to leave me at once, for your ideas and phantasies are but the illusions that creep like maggots into civilizations when they begin to decline, and into minds when they begin to decay.[8]

But Robartes and Aherne continued in attendance, waiting their opportunity, which came in 1917 when Yeats discovered what he was for a time to call their 'papers'. He went back over the old stories about them in the inductions to *A Vision*. By then it had all become precise:

'Have I proved that civilisations come to an end when they have given all their light like burned-out wicks, that ours is near its end?' 'Or transformation', Aherne corrected. [The narrator answers affirmatively.] 'If you had answered differently' said Robartes, 'I would have sent you away, for we are here to consider the terror that is to come.' [9]

The prophecies of destruction were now combined with the notion of the historical cycles, and there formed about them a rich cluster of attendant images: the annunciations, the 'rough beast' which is also demiurgic, the harlot of the new dispensation who supplants the virgin of the old. Catastrophe is everywhere interlocked with renewal, and accepted with terror and joy.[10]

This complex of ideas satisfied Yeats's desire to 'arrange in one clear view'. It contributed much to the force and splendour of a few poems such as 'The Second Coming', 'Leda and the Swan', and 'The Gyres', and in *The Resurrection* a part of it achieved theatrical expression. But the other plays in which Yeats sought to employ it are much less successful. Although he toiled at them arduously, neither *Where There Is Nothing*, nor *The Unicorn from the Stars* nor *The Player Queen* are as interesting as some of the plays into which Yeats put less of the persecuting abstracts. One inherent disadvantage of the theme, from the point of view of both playwright and storyteller, was its prophetic character. Where everything moves towards a measureless consummation that is to take place in the future, the characters tend to be reduced to evangelists and sectaries; and it is difficult for the divine event for which everyone is waiting to be wrought into the business of the stage. Even in *The Player Queen*, where Yeats had much success in turning his *preparatio* into an intrigue, the feeling that a good deal is necessarily withheld from the audience is frustrating when the last curtain falls. *The Resurrection* does not suffer from this because it is a history-play and it was possible to put into it the revelation towards which it builds.

In *Where There Is Nothing* (1903) Yeats to some extent overcame this difficulty by stressing the fortunes of the hero, who is another version of the outcasts in *The Secret Rose*. Paul Ruttledge is a celibate country gentleman who has begun to see his relatives and fellow-magistrates as just an ungenial collection of barnyard fowl. He has dreams of destruction in which he identifies himself with 'Laughter, the mightiest of the enemies of God'. It is a beast which he wishes to overtake, a 'very terrible wild beast, with iron teeth and brazen claws that root up spires and towers'.[11] After he has repudiated his old life and its established society and changed clothes with Charlie Ward the tinker we see him in the second Act a member of the tinkers' gang, learning from them and trying to teach them. Repudiating another worn-out emblem of civilization, he marries the tinker girl Sabina Silver by 'lepping over the tinkers' budget', and in the next Act demoralizes the whole village with free drink. This makes him very popular with the tinkers, but less so with the magistrates. When they attempt to put a stop to it all, Paul and the tinkers seize them and subject them to a mock trial:

You have come into a different kingdom now; the old kingdom of the people of the roads, the houseless people. We call ourselves tinkers, and you are going to put us on our trial if you can. You call yourselves Christians and we will put you on your trial first.[12]

All the Christian magistrates are convicted of 'breaking the doctrine they boast of'. At the beginning of the fourth Act the tinkers take Paul, who is ill, to be looked after in a monastery. Five years pass, and he has become an heretical monk and has acquired a few disciples. Emerging from a trance, he preaches a sermon to them —a portion of the play that gave Yeats much trouble—in which the history of mankind is sketched as a gradual decline from God-given joyous impulse to a society immured by institutions and victimized by 'all the animal spirits that have loved things better than life'. But 'the Christian must live so that all things shall pass away':

We must destroy the World; we must destroy everything that has Law and Number, for where there is nothing, there is God.[13]

Banished from the monastery, his teaching beyond the grasp of his own disciples (who wish to re-create institutions in order to live in greater comfort), Paul at length dies at the hands of a superstitious mob.

Una Ellis-Fermor found much to admire in both the characterization and the sentiments of *Where There Is Nothing*.[14] In a play whose design is that of the life-story everything seems to depend upon what the playwright achieves with his protagonist. Neither Yeats nor his collaborators (Douglas Hyde and Lady Gregory) were able to make Paul Ruttledge potent or interesting enough. There are moments when he is talking to Father Jerome in the first Act and to Charlie Ward and the other tinkers in the second Act when it seems as though he may be coming to life. These are some of the quieter passages in the play, and Paul's animation is agreeably correlated with the growing signs of affectionate puzzlement or respectful tolerance that the other persons feel for him. Paul, too, is successfully kept in the centre of the action; as rebel, as teacher, and as victim he seems to have the possibility of complex life. But all is vitiated by his inexpressiveness. Unprovided with either friend or foe, he is a Richard without Buckingham, or without the soliloquies. He is surrounded by lifeless people. The curse of this play, as of several others, is Yeats's taste for hosts of minor characters; the more they crowd the scene, the more they drain the life from it. Paul can address them only in a public voice, with sentiments out of Blake, Nietzsche, and Tolstoy. But this eloquence is unpersuasive because it proceeds from a character who gives us so little of his own inner travail. To Yeats himself Paul soon appeared to be 'arid and dominating'. The play's faults of construction, such as the clumsy attempt to solder the break between the tinker's camp and the monastery, do not need emphasis.

Where There Is Nothing was hurriedly put together by the three collaborators 'spurred by an external necessity' (which was the fear that George Moore would steal the plot).[15] It was admired by many people, including Shaw. Yeats himself repudiated it, partly because of its faults of construction and its unsympathetic hero, partly because of what he came to consider the 'crude speculative commonplaces' of the 'trial'-scene in Act III, and he would not allow Bullen to reprint it in the Stratford edition,[16] where it was replaced by Lady Gregory's new version of the theme, *The Unicorn from the Stars* (1908). The collaborators have reduced the tangled life-story of Paul Ruttledge to a single action: Martin Hearne's vision of the trampling unicorn, the fabulous beast whose destruction of the old order fills Martin with joyful terror, his entanglement with the outlaws who interpret his teaching in acts of drunken anarchy that terrify all the respectable folk, and his final vision, before he is shot in a scuffle with the constables, that the battle of ruin and rebirth is to be fought in the human mind, in mental fight:

MARTIN

It was but a frenzy, that going out to burn and to destroy. What have I do with the foreign army? What I have to pierce is the wild heart of time. My business is not reformation but revelation.

JOHNNY

If you are going to turn back now from leading us, you are no better than any other traitor that ever gave up the work he took in hand. Let you come and face now the two hundred men you brought out daring the power of the law last night, and give them your reason for failing them.

MARTIN

I was mistaken when I set out to destroy Church and Law. The battle we have to fight is fought out in our own mind. There is a fiery moment, perhaps once in a lifetime, and in that moment we see the only thing that matters. It is in that moment the great battles are lost and won, for in that moment we are a part of the host of heaven.[17]

In *The Unicorn from the Stars* the symbolism is much more coherent and meaningful. Martin's destruction of the golden state-coach which he has been building is the poet's destruction of his own artefact, the deed which chooses that 'heavenly mansion', 'perfection of the life' and not of the work;[18] yet it proceeds with substantial realism from the coachbuilder's artisan that he is in the

play. The reduction of the visionary's rank from country gentleman to tradesman resulted in further unities of setting and society.
It was in the development of Martin's two uncles and of Father
John that Lady Gregory showed most skill. Thomas Hearne, the
respectable coachbuilder, is much more actual than the ninepins
which Paul Ruttledge knocks over, and in Father John and the
second uncle, Andrew Hearne, the possibilities of Thomas Ruttledge and Father Jerome in *Where There Is Nothing* are effectively
developed. They are men who, through learning or tempera-
ment or both, have themselves experienced something of Martin's
visionary turbulence; they exemplify those 'strange souls born
everywhere to-day', of whom Yeats wrote in *The Trembling of
the Veil*, 'with hearts that Christianity, as shaped by history, cannot satisfy'.[19] They help the audience to believe in and sympathize
with Martin. There is no doubt that in so decisively preferring
The Unicorn from the Stars to its earlier version Yeats showed sound
judgement as a theatrical craftsman.

II

Yeats's note on *The Player Queen* explains a good deal about its
origin and theme:

I began in, I think, 1907, a verse tragedy, but at that time the thought
I have set forth in *Per Amica Silentia Lunae* was coming into my head,
and I found examples of it everywhere. I wasted the best working
months of several years in an attempt to write a poetical play where
every character became an example of the finding or not finding of
what I have called the Antithetical Self; and because passion and not
thought makes tragedy, what I made had neither simplicity nor life.
... At last it came into my head all of a sudden that I could get rid of
the play if I turned it into a farce; and never did I do anything so easily,
for I think that I wrote the present play in about a month.[20]

Yeats's doctrine of the Mask, the notion that each man can find
his hidden opposite, his anti- (or antithetical) self, is his best-
known 'myth'. The mask of the anti-self, to be sought out with
courage, is worn by those 'who are no longer deceived, whose
passion is reality';[21] * it bring happiness:

* The last phrase appears, from its context, to mean 'who have a passion
for (specifically) religious truth'.

all happiness depends on the energy to assume the mask of some other life, on a re-birth as something not one's self, something created in a moment and perpetually renewed.

The finding of the Mask is one of Martin Hearne's 'fiery moments'; the wearing of it at last defines what Owen Aherne meant by saying 'I must become completely alive'. Another passage in *Per Amica* bears directly on *The Player Queen*:

When I had this thought I could see nothing else in life. I could not write the play I had planned, for all became allegorical, and though I tore up hundreds of pages in my endeavour to escape from allegory, my imagination became sterile for nearly five years and I only escaped at last when I had mocked in a comedy my own thought.[22]

In *The Player Queen* the finding of a Mask is linked to the miraculous end of an era and the coming of a new dispensation—all that is symbolized in *Where There Is Nothing* by the beast with iron claws and in *The Unicorn from the Stars* by the trampling, milk-white unicorn. The combined themes are transformed into Yeats's nearest approach to a neo-classical comedy of sexual intrigue. The poet, teacher, victim, and evangelist divide into a humour-character and a grotesque, while other grotesques abound. The setting is removed from Ireland to a nameless country whose only visible political institutions are a queen, a mob, and a comic prime minister. By these means Yeats's thought is made to dance in a sufficiently gay and extraordinary fashion.

To mock one's own thought is not ncessarily to achieve an escape from allegory; it need not mean more than the substitution of a comic allegory for a serious one. By altering the temper and tone of his chosen images (putting, for example, a silly goose like the Queen in *The Player Queen* into the place of a tragedy-queen) Yeats may have hoped to transform the thought into comedy and so escape from its sombre and exalted appeal, which threatened to become a persecuting obsession. In the essays on Blake and on 'The Symbolism of Poetry' Yeats had long before suggested that thought and image can and should be wrought into symbol; and perhaps, if that is done, then all that is needed to mock one's thought is to transform the symbol. Yeats may have considered that a transformation of that kind was at work when he re-wrote the play as a comedy. We must grant that Yeats did not wish merely to present the old, sombre notions dressed up in gladder rags. But it is doubtful whether thought and image had been wholly wrought into symbol. The transformation, since it is only a comicalizing of the image, leaves the basic tone and temper of the thought unaffected, and perhaps the relation between image, character, and story on the one hand and the persecuting abstract on the other remains essentially akin to that which obtains in allegory. Comic character and behaviour and all that is meant by the development of an intrigue, at least, although they may be intended to convey by what they are and do the meanings that are being mocked, still contain patches of uneasiness and of great obscurity.

Some of the qualities of *The Player Queen* give evidence of the survival of old perplexities. First, there is some inconsistency in the method of characterization and the behaviour of individual characters; sometimes they play intelligible roles in a comic matter which does convey its own meaning, sometimes their gestures or concernments fail to convey meaning to any but the most initiated spectator (who has to go outside the play for a gloss).[23] Secondly, some of the implications of the story have a melancholy resonance which is out of accord with the impudent events and the farcical fortunes. It begs the question to declare that the clothes are gay but that *au fond* the spirit is grave, but there is more than a hint of bitter conclusions which suggest that Yeats had not really succeeded in mocking his own thought. There are strange inconstancies of tone, which may derive from uncertainty—the author's uncertainty unconsciously betrayed to the spectator— about the genre. The 'comedy' is a 'farce' as well, and a farce, Yeats reminded Lady Gregory, is 'comedy with character left out'. But character, in the sense of the discrimination and definition of individuality, is no more absent from *The Player Queen* than it was absent from *Deirdre*. In this respect, *The Player Queen* fits Yeats's definition of farce no better than *Deirdre* fitted his definition of tragedy. Perhaps we should be content to call it a tragi-comedy: a label which is unsatisfactory only because Yeats would have regarded it as a contradiction in terms.

There are, as Becker has pointed out, two stories in the play. They are carefully interwoven, one being centred on Septimus the drunken poet and the other on his wife Decima the player

queen. They are members of a company of players which has
arrived at the castle of the Queen and is to perform, by order of
her Prime Minister, a play called *The Tragical History of Noah's
Deluge*. The first Act belongs mainly to Septimus. He is a comic
poète maudit and parodies the central characters in the *Secret Rose*
stories; his drunkenness is a literalized and comical version of the
spiritual intoxication of Paul Ruttledge and Martin Hearne,
drunk with the grapes of wrath. Like them, he has his vision: of
the chaste, noble, and religious unicorn, the 'hidden, flying image'
of all that he is not, his Mask. His 'humour' is to make tipsy
speeches about it in enamelled rhetoric. Before he stumbles on
to the stage looking for his wife Decima, whose disappearance
threatens the performance of the morrow's play, two old men
have been commenting on the disturbance made by rioters in
the night-time streets. Septimus's quarrel with the two 'bad, popular poets' whom he encounters (as they are returning apparently
from a brothel) underlines his role as a proud outcast. He goes to
sleep in the gutter, but is disturbed by a crowd of citizens who are
rioting against the Queen. They say that she has never been seen
outside her castle during the seven years of her reign; she must be
a bad, evil-living witch; there is a story told by a goat-herd who
looked through her window and saw her coupling with a great
white unicorn, which on another occasion he shot at and wounded.
Septimus gets up to defend the chastity of the unicorn, but is
soon knocked down by one of the peasants, who have decided
to break into the castle and strangle the Queen. Then the crowds
disappear when the Old Beggar is reported to be coming in their
direction. The Old Beggar is a grotesque parody of the evangelist
who announces the new dispensation. His back begins to itch, he
looks for straw to lie upon, and brays like a donkey every time
the crown changes. His back is itching now, he explains to Septimus, and poet and evangelist go off the stage together.

This Act is clearly an ingeniously contrived preparation for
what is to come. The parodic roles of poet and prophet are obvious, although the characters are of different types—one is purely
a symbolic grotesque, the other is a comic humour-character.
Similar matchings occur in some of Jonson's plays and seem
awkward there too. The audience is presumably expected to
wait patiently or eagerly for the mystery of the unicorn to be

disclosed: which is right about it, Septimus or the crowd, and are they talking about the same thing? But the crowd itself dashes the comedy down into ugliness and bestiality. Their superstitious brutality and gloating chatter about the strangling of witches show that Yeats has not been able to rid his imagination of the tempestuous squalor that accompanies the falling-apart of an old era as the new one approaches. Here the tone of comedy is lost.

The second Act opens with an angry Prime Minister demanding that the missing Decima be found:

> I know her sort; would pull the world to pieces to spite her husband or her lover. I know her—a bladder full of dried peas for a brain, a brazen, bragging baggage.[24]

This splutter is interrupted by the entrance of the Queen. She is a nun-like creature, ascetic and badly dressed, devoted to Holy Saint Octema, and has reluctantly agreed to show herself to her people, although quite persuaded that this will result in her martyrdom at their hands:

> I have now attained to the age of my patroness, Holy Saint Octema, when she was martyred at Antioch. You will remember that her unicorn was so pleased at the spectacle of her austerity that he caracoled in his excitement. Thereupon she dropped out of the saddle and was trampled to death under the feet of the mob. Indeed, but for the unicorn, the mob would have killed her long before.

The unicorn is still an emblem of destruction, although the Queen does not recognize this. What is to her symbolic union with an image of chastity and austerity is bestial witchcraft to the brutish crowd and supplies the main reason why they wish to kill her as the Saint was killed. This seems to be an attempt, though not perhaps a very successful one, to turn the unicorn into a comic or ironic antinomy.

The Prime Minister despairs of ever making the Queen appear sufficiently queenly; she is utterly unfitted for her role in life and seeks only to run away to a convent. But he has a plan, as yet undisclosed, that will make her acceptable to the people. When they go off the stage, Nona, the other leading actress of the company, appears with a lobster and a bottle of wine and lures the hungry Decima from her hiding-place under the throne.

What follows is a long, rapidly developed scene of comic

intrigue, with Decima as the heroine of more than a comedy of humours. She refuses to play the part allotted to her in *The Tragical History of Noah's Deluge* (an old tale of the destruction, or preservation, of the world), in which she has been cast for the role of that old harridan Noah's wife, whom 'a foul husband beats with a stick because she won't clamber among the other brutes into his cattleboat'. In refusing to wear the mask of this brutish role she seeks one antithetical to it: 'the only part in the world I can play is a great Queen's part'. Nona replies scornfully:

You play a Queen's part? You that were born in a ditch between two towns and wrapped in a sheet that was stolen from a hedge.

Thus in Decima there are interwoven from her first appearance her two roles as a 'ditch-delivered drab' and as an artist or heroine seeking her anti-self. Her song, which she attributes to the 'mad singing-daughter of a harlot', combines these two subjects, as well as the theme of the sexual conjunction of woman and bird as it appears in 'Leda and the Swan', the symbolic poem concerned with the annunciation to Leda that 'founded Greece' and was followed next in the series by the annunciation made to the virgin that founded Christendom.[25]

> She pulled the thread and bit the thread
> And made a golden gown,
> She wept because she had dreamt that I
> Was born to wear a crown.
>
> 'When she was got,' my mother sang,
> 'I heard a seamew cry,
> I saw a flake of yellow foam
> That dropped upon my thigh.'

The significance of the Harlot as the 'virgin' of the post-Christian annunciation has been explained by Giorgio Melchiori and by F. A. C. Wilson, chiefly by collating it with Yeats's story 'The Adoration of the Magi', a first version of which appeared in 1897. This story is about a Parisian prostitute, who is visited by the Three Wise Men, those Magi who, in the poem of that title, are 'by Calvary's turbulence unsatisfied'.[26] In the 1925 version of this story the girl gives birth to a 'cold, hard, and virginal unicorn', the emblem of the new era.[27]

It may fairly be claimed that in *The Player Queen* itself Yeats leaves this aspect of Decima impenetrably obscure. William Becker, who praised the play as a 'clear candidate for popular acceptance' (because its meaning emerges through its dramatic context), missed the aspect of Decima as Harlot, because he did not make the necessary connexion with 'Leda and the Swan' and 'The Adoration of the Magi'. It is therefore all the harder to see how any audience could penetrate so far, except the group to whom Yeats dedicated *Reveries over Childhood and Youth*: 'those few people mainly personal friends who have read all that I have written'.[28]

Yeats indeed shaped his second Act round another subject. He concentrated on the process whereby Decima is stripped of everything in the old life so that she may live the new one. By this method the material becomes human comedy, for the process is rendered as a traditional intrigue, although the theme itself is constantly recurring in Yeats, and is seriously treated in *The Hour-Glass*, *Where There Is Nothing*, and elsewhere:

To seek God too soon is not less sinful than to seek God too late; we must love man, woman or child, we must exhaust ambition, intellect, desire, dedicating all things as they pass, or we come to God with empty hands.[29]

Decima loses her man Septimus and her part in *The Tragical History* to Nona. In passages where the two women needle each other jealously about their hold over Septimus, Nona reveals that Septimus is her lover and that she was in bed with him when Septimus composed the verses to Decima which Decima carries next to her heart. Decima therefore feels, or pretends to feel, free to choose a new man. When the players come in, dressed for their animal parts in the Noah play—Bull and Turkey are the two animals mentioned, the first combining (being a pantomimic bull) two men—she considers their possibilities, and then all the players dance while she sings about Pasiphae and Leda:

> Spring and straddle, stride and strut,
> Shall I choose a bird or brute?
> Name the feather or the fur
> For my single comforter?

According to Wilson, this is a dance of 'sexual invitation to Godhead',[30] and this is what we might expect of the Harlot/Leda of the new annunciation. But it seems capable of being interpreted in another way: as just as much an emblem of her old life as it is of the new one that is being prepared for her. For what else is her choice amongst the player-beasts but another attempt to 'clamber among the other brutes into [Noah's] cattle-boat'? The farmyard animals are analogous to the barnyard creatures in *Where There Is Nothing* whom Paul Ruttledge actualizes in nightmare and in topiary-work,[31] and eventually repudiates. Certainly, from the position of this episode in *The Player Queen* it is a fair inference that during it Decima is still clinging to the old life, because, although she has ostensibly given Septimus up, she none the less tries desperately to keep him in the next part of the scene. The point is left obscure because the dance is broken off when Septimus comes in.

He is still half-drunk, has much in mind the impatient mob gathering outside the castle, and is radiant with a new idea about the unicorn:

I announce the end of the Christian Era, the coming of a New Dispensation, that of the New Adam, that of the Unicorn; but alas, he is chaste, he hesitates, he hesitates. . . . I will fail upon the Unicorn for his chastity. I will bid him trample mankind to death and beget a new race.

Here Seanchan's Nietzschean race of the future and Martin Hearne's unicorn of destruction have bcome assimilated to the godhead as beast, and to the theme of the anti-self. As Melchiori explains the latter point:

The Unicorn is chastity itself. Copulation and begetting are its opposite, its Mask. Now, the consummation by the Unicorn of an act of lust would mean reaching its own opposite, its Mask; and this is outside the range of natural possibilities, it is miracle . . . Only miracle can produce the end of an era and the advent of a New Dispensation.[32]

But so far as the action of this play is concerned, the change of crowns itself is effected not by miracle but by the development of the story of Decima as a personage in a comic intrigue.

She does her best to retain Septimus ('If you would be faithful to me, Septimus, I would not let a man of them touch me'), but Septimus eventually follows Nona out through the door that Decima has locked, but of which Nona has recaptured the key.

Septimus is characterized as a man who knows the truth, but lacks courage and energy for the measureless consummation. He piles the images of his art upon his back, and chooses a woman who is not, as Decima is, 'terrible' to him,[33] and takes flight from the wrath to come, carrying in his hand the high-crowned hat of Noah the preserver. At the same time he has had his vision. He still dreams that he will aid the unicorn to accomplish its anti-self and become the image to which man may unite himself (the theme of Byzantium, and the Byzantium poems).

When we have put all in safety we will go to the high tablelands of Africa and find where the Unicorn is stabled and sing a marriage song. I will stand before the terrible blue eye.

But 'putting all [the properties of *The Tragical History*] in safety' is hardly compatible with surrender to the apocalypse, and the unicorn is conveniently remote. He will never visit the unicorn but will continue to dream about it, a *poète maudit* to the end, who, by renouncing Decima, unintentionally leaves her free to accomplish her destiny. Irony engulfs him. He is at bottom a tragic figure; he both withdraws from the heart of the story (the life of Decima) and is extruded by it. All his comic drunkard's rhetoric does not conceal this, but allows us to perceive the difference between gay clothes and the frustrated hero, a Cuchulain of the poetic life.

Decima is now completely deserted, and when the Old Beggar enters, still looking for his straw, she is thinking about plunging the wardrobe-mistress's scissors into her breast. He urges her not to, and gives her a glimpse of the life after death which takes away the last hope and curiously controverts the substance of *The Dreaming of the Bones* and *Purgatory*:

DECIMA

I have been betrayed by a man, I have been made a mockery of. Do those who are dead, old man, make love and do they find good lovers?

OLD BEGGAR

I will whisper you another secret. People talk, but I have never known anything to come from there but an old jackass. Maybe there is nothing else. Who knows but he has the whole place to himself?

This perhaps is 'mocking one's own thought', but we can see that the result is not necessarily gay. Reduced to this gloomy and empty vision, Decima is about to stab herself: 'a hero loves the world till it breaks him'.[34]

Then the Queen comes in. They quickly agree to change clothes and roles; Decima finds her Mask in a flash. This is a point on the play where the λύσις, the sudden untying of the tangled skein traditional in neo-classical comedy, perfectly matches the thought, for the Mask is found 'in a moment', one of Martin Hearne's 'fiery moments': 'the antithetical man works by flashes of lightning'.[35] Decima assumes the Queen's role expecting to die in her stead at the hands of the mob:

O, your Majesty, I shall die whatever you do, and if only I could wear that gold brocade and those gold slippers for one moment, it would not be so hard to die.

For she has become 'completely alive'.

It is difficult to be sure what mood dominates at the end of the play and whether or not all the preceding themes achieve completion and resolution there, although events can be clearly set down. The Prime Minister comes back, after he has disclosed to the mob the plan to save the situation that he had mentioned earlier to the Queen: it is that he should marry her. This has kept the people quiet—in Act I a citizen had cried, 'When [the Queen] is dead we will make the Prime Minister King.' He is amazed to find Decima in the Queen's place, but she can play the role as though she had been born to it (as indeed she has). Her majestic beauty instantaneously overawes crowd and Minister, who begins to desire her. The bray of a donkey is heard and the Beggar-evangelist is dragged in. He is packed off to prison as an impostor, for it is now policy to maintain that the real Queen has not disappeared and that the crown has not changed hands; Septimus (who ineffectually attempts to disclose the truth) and the other players who know who the new Queen really is are expelled from the kingdom. In the revised edition (1934) Decima addresses them in a farewell speech; during it, both symbolically and for the purposes of disguise, she wears the mask of the sister of Noah who in *The Tragical History* had refused to enter his 'cattle-boat' and had been drowned in the flood of destruction.

The ending is comic in so far as Decima finds her Mask, and happiness; the donkey's bray and the mask of Noah's sister make it plain that the crown has truly changed, and that a new dispensation has arrived. But the annunciation is kept secret and ironically muddled; the Prime Minister takes various measures to conceal what has really happened, as does Decima herself, and the crowds that acclaim her are utterly deceived, for they suppose that the new Queen is only their old one writ finer than they had expected and are unaware that their revolt against their chaste and virginal ruler because of her imputed witchcraft and harlotry has landed them with a witch and harlot indeed.

Decima's status as harlot of the new annunciation seems, as before, a matter which can hardly be explained without external aid. F. A. C. Wilson is prepared to make the necessary inference: 'We are left to infer that the form in which divinity is to descend to Decima is that of the unicorn, the disguise under which it manifests in this palace.'[36] This may be right, but one of the objections to it is that throughout the play the unicorn in its aspect of immanent beast-deity is the property of Septimus's imagination and has, as it were, gone off with him when he withdrew from the story. Decima, after all, does not marry a unicorn, or even talk about one; she marries the Prime Minister, who has been ruling the kingdom for seven years already. It is true that his reign appears to be over, since it is apparent that Decima will stand no nonsense from him; but what is this farcical figure doing in the new era? He proposes, suggests Wilson, to 'usurp the function of Godhead',[37] and this sounds much more like the real ending. But you cannot easily have it both ways: Decima cannot be both the bride of God and the bride of his usurper; and if Yeats is hinting that the Prime Minister is to be God's unwitting surrogate, like Congal and his men in *The Herne's Egg*, the theme is so darkly rendered in *The Player Queen* as to require exegesis from a sequel written fourteen years later. It may be, finally, that it is by means of this episode that the sense in which the play is the farce that Yeats called it is made most plain. Decima, expecting death, finds instead her anti-self and her happiness; but a condition of this seems to be that she must unite herself with a buffoon. Below the farce, as is the case with Septimus's drunken rhetoric, there lurks the hint of tragedy.

On various grounds, then, *The Player Queen* seems an imperfect achievement, if we attempt to judge it as the comedy Yeats thought he had written. The point is worth making boldly, in view of the tendency amongst recent commentators to single it out for special approval. The great interest of the play is, of course, Decima; she is the new Deirdre and was, if allegory had not frustrated all, to be her successor in the repertoire of Mrs. Patrick Campbell; like Deirdre she had the courage and 'energy of soul' to assume the role that would alter her story after the bitter experience of playing parts devised for others' stories; and like Deirdre she achieves her imaginative triumph in the face of death. For Deirdre's stately passions are not merely 'mocked' and 'got rid of' by Decima's wit and sensuality. The resemblance, as well as the difference, between the pair are the index of a vast, potential enlargement of the woman's place in Yeats's drama—the shadowing forth of a figure various enough to comprise both Deirdre and Crazy Jane. Such a figure, Yeats's unwritten Cleopatra, did not after all appear, and the more's the pity if Decima was, as we may suspect, the original impulse of *The Player Queen* when it was started shortly after the success of *Deirdre* and proceeded to run foul, as we have seen, of the 'persecution of the abstract'.

It is probably this persecution that makes it, despite the liveliness and assurance of its writing and characterization and the highly successful scene of neo-classical comedy between Nona and Decima, inferior to works on a much more modest scale such as *Purgatory*. 'Aesthetically speaking', Professor Edgar Wind has said, 'there can be no doubt that the presence of unresolved residues of meaning is an obstacle to the enjoyment of art.' [38] It is still possible for a commentator, to offer an account of the play by freely interpreting its character and plot and disregarding its theme and history.[39] But most spectators are likely to keep restlessly enquiring 'Now what exactly does the playwright mean by *that*?' Too often the answers cannot be provided from the play itself. Apart from the larger problems, some of which I have discussed, there is a continuous spray of surface detail which it is not impertinent to call substantially allegorical still. This at least seems to make *The Player Queen* a poor choice for an audience that expects meanings to be conveyed through the dramatic context.

III

In November, 1935, Yeats wrote to Dorothy Wellesley about his new play, 'as wild a play as *Player Queen*, as amusing but more tragedy and philosophic depth'. Originally planned as a three-act tragedy, it eventually became *The Herne's Egg*, in six Scenes, 'the strangest wildest thing I have ever written'.[40]

The animal presences and the sexual themes are responsible for the first impressions of strangeness. There is much that seems like the games of children—the stylized battles, Corney scolding his life-size toy-donkey, the village-children catechizing Attracta, Congal's six child-like men—and this is oddly conjoined with the sexual theme, rape and the sacred marriage. *The Herne's Egg* is crowded and stagy, too, not a play for the drawing-room, but more on the scale of the old Abbey plays and *The Player Queen*, with its different locations, its fourteen speaking parts, and an abundance of properties and stage-effects. The absence of a chorus brings us face to face with a protagonist in a way that had scarcely been attempted since *The King's Threshold*, except in *The Player Queen* itself. These piquant contrasts and lavish arrangements to some extent conceal a concern, similar to that in the Cuchulain plays, with the working out of an individualized hero's destiny and with a fable which is almost as regular as one of Ovid's: a man commits sacrilege against a god by stealing his sacred objects and violating his priestess, and is suitably punished with metamorphosis. Yeats gives this ancient tale of mortal hubris and divine implacability 'philosophic depth' by making his hero's stubbornness an intransigent assertion of his human self and un-christened heart. Congal claims.

> as by a soldier's right
> A charter to commit the crime once more.

What makes Congal's story complex and ironically determines the nature of his struggle is that he does not understand the god against whom he makes war. It is made plain in the play that this failure of understanding is inseparable from his role as man, sol-dier, and chieftain. The bird-god, the Great Herne, is known only to his initiate the priestess Attracta. Congal is precluded by all that he is, by every occasion on which he employs the weapons of his manhood, from being an initiate. He is therefore different from Cuchulain or Emer, who know what they contend with, even when it is supernatural. The god in *The Herne's Egg* can terrify but not convert Congal. The hero fighting the god under these conditions is also a kind of fool; when he releases his grip on the life he lives, he is turned into a donkey. It is in accord with this that Congal should be set in the context of much brash and oafish life, and that events and properties should seem to mock at him. The contrast between this element and Attracta's exalted and sacerdotal role enforces the theme as well as the vitality of the play.

In the first Scene Congal, King of Connaught, and Aedh, King of Tara, conclude a peace after their fiftieth drawn battle. Theirs has been a prelapsarian world, like Red Hanrahan's Heaven, whose music was the 'continual clashing of swords'. In the next Scene Congal and his men visit the abode of the Great Herne, where lives the promised bride of the god. They pillage the eggs from the hernery as a delicacy for the supper at Tara which is to celebrate the peace. This act is at first largely unmotivated, the impulse without which the play cannot move, but it soon assumes a different character. Congal behaves as an unbeliever in the face of the god's and his priestess's claim. Must old campaigners forego a delicacy because

a woman thinks that she
Is promised or married to a bird?[41]

Attracta's marriage to the god is a perverted fancy arising from frustration:

Women thrown into despair
By the winter of their virginity
Take its abominable snow,
As boys take common snow, and make
An image of god or bird or beast
To feed their sensuality.

The cure for this condition is the experience of human sexuality. Happiness, replies Attracta, is to be found only in communion with the god: 'There is no happiness but the Great Herne'; but

Congal denies her right to say so, because she does not know what human pleasure is:

> pick,
> Or be picked by seven men,
> And we shall talk it out again.

Similarly, when the curse is pronounced upon him, that he must be changed into a fool and die at a fool's hand, it means nothing to him:

> That I shall live and die a fool,
> And die upon some battlefield
> At a fool's hand, is but natural,
> And needs no curse to bring it.

The saving clause 'upon some battlefield' shows the degree of his misunderstanding; he easily twists the sinister literalism of *fool* in the curse into a harmless, worldly generality. In all this, Congal blunts the supernatural by interpreting the signs of its immanence rationally and psychologically. Nothing in his conduct so far suggests that making war on the god would make sense to him.

When Congal and his men go, the audience is brought closer to the reality he has disregarded by Attracta's discourse on her mysterious marriage, addressed to the girls. They describe her trance. The priestess becomes the instrument of the god, vacated of all human will; she goes away carrying the hen's egg, which she has taken from one of the girls' baskets, and which is to destroy the harmony of Congal's life and initiate the curse. The god is present when his tune 'The Great Herne's Feather' is played, and in Scene iii, before the gates of Tara, the Great Herne flies over Congal's troop while they try to stone and slash him, taking him more for an angry bird than for an enraged divinity. And then (Scene iv) Congal bursts from the feast at Tara in a drunken rage, accusing Aedh of having insulted him by substituting a hen's egg for the hernes' eggs which every other man has had. Since they have given up their arms, the two kings fight with legs broken from the tables, and Congal kills Aedh, bringing to an end the condition of heroic equilibrium which they enjoyed before the curse began:

> I would not have had him die that way
> Or die at all, he should have been immortal.
> Our fifty battles had made us friends.

And there are fifty more to come.
New weapons, a new leader will be found
And everything begin again.

MIKE

Much bloodier.

CONGAL

They had, we had
Forgotten what we fought about,
So fought like gentlemen, but now
Knowing the truth must fight like beasts.

Congal acknowledges his Fall. The truth that they know is certainly not any mystical truth acquired through the consumption of the sacred eggs (which anyway no one will have had time to consume), but the 'truth' about war as hatred ending in death, not a gentlemanly contest between equally matched technicians; it is something which is not 'legal' and is 'bloody'. Congal guesses at why it has all happened:

Maybe the Great Herne's curse has done it.
Why not? Answer me that; why not?

This is Congal's first acknowledgement of the god's comminatory power over him, and it is followed by the entry of Attracta, still entranced and carrying the missing herne's egg that should have been on Congal's plate. Her presence and her continued possession by the god are the sign that what now happens is his will. The troopers realize the part she has played and wish to take their revenge, but in a manner consonant with their claim to be gentlemen. As James says,

All that have done what she did must die,
But, in a manner of speaking, pleasantly,
Because legally, certainly not
By beating with a table-leg.

When Mike reminds Congal that Attracta is dedicated to the god, James's argument is reinterpreted in an important speech by Congal. It sums up what he has learnt from the experience so far,

acknowledging the god's handiwork and introducing the theme
of the war against god for the first time:

> I had forgotten
> That all she does he makes her do,
> But he is god and out of reach;
> Nor stone can bruise, nor a sword pierce him,
> And yet through his betrothed, his bride,
> I have the power to make him suffer;
> His curse has given me the right,
> I am to play the fool and die
> At a fool's hands.

The difference between dying like a fool 'upon some battlefield'
and *playing the fool* shows how far Congal's acknowledgements
have carried him.

He constitutes himself a court, and decides that the seven men
shall violate the priestess 'in the name of the law'. It is to be a
'pleasant' and 'legal' undertaking, an attempt to recapture the
prelapsarian equilibrium, a refusal to accept the bloody and illegal
irrationality which has crumbled away the old heaven. When his
followers hesitate, he reproves them:

> Whoever disobeys the Court
> Is an unmannerly, disloyal lout,
> And no good citizen.

For 'A Court of Law is a blessed thing' and 'everything out of
balance accursed':

> When the Court decides on a decree
> Men carry it out with dignity.

The restoration of psychological balance is also reasserted and
earlier definitions of it maintained when Congal claims that the
violation will do 'a great good' for Attracta:

> Melting out the virgin snow,
> And that snow image, the Great Herne;
> . . . when it melts
> She may, being free from all obsession,
> Live as every woman should.

At the end of the scene, Attracta's song, as she stands motionless in her trance, affirms as a contravention of all this the mystery and unreason of the divine marriage.

In this scene Congal's 'law' itself may be read as the consequence of his fall into disorder and hence as incompetent to restore the old equilibrium. Attracta's condition during it, furthermore, suggests that all he does is done at the god's behest, that he is already playing the fool, ironically unaware that law and reason and revenge against the god are simply the motives that the Great Herne uses to effect his own end, which is the consummation of the marriage.

But, as the play develops, the stress falls more on Congal's stubborn refusal, or inability, to judge his own acts as other than they seem to him, and on his continuing conviction, despite his terror, that he can of his own choice fight the god who (to another than Congal—the audience, for example) appears to determine everything the hero does, even his fighting. Thus Congal resembles one of those Renaissance perspective toys where the shape seen depends upon the angle of vision. He is one way a fool; but another way, because the understanding that the audience has of the rigidly god-determined world in which he lives is withheld from him, a hero asserting his freedom and selfhood against the thunder and the curse.

This works out in the two remaining Scenes. When Scene v begins Congal thinks that he has proved a point: Attracta has been done great good:

> No more a herne's bride, a crazed loony,
> Waiting to be trodden by a bird,
> But all woman, sensible woman.

Corroboration is to hand in the claim of the six other men; they have indeed lain with the priestess. Attracta affirms that 'My husband came to me in the night', and in response to her prayer the round heaven declares in thunder that the darling of the god is 'pure'. The terrified men, all except Congal, proceed to retract:

MATHIAS

> I was a fool to believe myself
> When everybody knows that I am a liar.

151

Attracta threatens them with punishment for what they have said (not for what they have done): after death they will all be changed into gross animal-shapes; the thunder is heard again, confirming the sentence. This drives even Congal to his knees, but not to retraction:

> I held you in my arms last night,
> We seven held you in our arms.

Unlike Mathias, Congal must believe himself. This is an aspect of his heroic selfhood. And what he says is true, for the mystery of the sacred bride-bed is that the men have acted as the surrogates of the god. Therefore Attracta is also right in her claim that she has suffered no violation. This mystery Congal cannot perceive. He fights an enemy whose absolute power he comes to acknowledge but whose mystery is hidden from him. But the fight is a real one to him and makes the sort of heroic sense which he understands—the untamed self striving against supernatural odds. As long as he remains a hero, he can see his relationship with god as a fight with him, though in the god's perspective it can be no such thing, but only a rigid sequence of offence and punishment. Congal heroically rationalizes this sequence as a series of bouts with the god, which he thinks he can win or lose. This is his way of saying in his own language how he lives; he is not to know that it somewhat imperfectly expresses his place in the macrocosmic rationale.

Throughout the play the offence has been the theft of the hernes' eggs. This has to work itself out through the fulfilment of the original curse ('And to end his fool breath / At a fool's hand meet his death') before the punishment for 'saying' that he has lain with the priestess is brought to bear. In the last Scene Congal is alone on the mountainside with Tom the Fool, a grotesque creature out of the kitchen, armed with a spit and the lid of a cauldron. This Fool, although he is sent by the god (he whistles 'The Great Herne's Feather'), is picturesquely incompetent, and Congal does not really expect to die at his hands. But now he sees the situation as the last of his three bouts with the god:

> He won the first, I won the second,
> Six men and I possessed his wife.
> . . . she said that nobody had touched her,

And after that the thunder said the same,
Yet I had won that bout, and now
I know that I shall win the third.

The first bout was the fall into disorder and the death of Aedh,
and the second the violation of Attracta. Thus Congal asserts to
the end what is true to the self and the senses, unable to see the
mystery of the rape that is a sacred marriage. He re-asserts also his
claim to have made the god 'suffer', although he no longer talks
rationally and psychologically, because now the god's terribleness
is fully known to him—what began as disregard ends as defiance
—and he has a nightmare vision of the Great Herne's implacability
when he thinks of the endless, sinister carnival of Fools that will be
sent up against him:

> And I, moon-crazed, moon-blind,
> Fighting and wounded, wounded and fighting.
> I never thought of such an end.

The war against the god is very different from the heroic battlefield.

This curse is not to be evaded unless the hero himself can disrupt
its cruel logic. This is the way in which Congal is to win and lose
his last bout:

> though I shall die
> I shall not die at a Fool's hand . . .
> If I should give myself a wound,
> Let life run away, I'd win the bout.

Then the thought strikes him:

> Fool! Am I myself a Fool?
> For if I am a Fool, he wins the bout.

His answer is, like 'I am Duchess of Malfi still', a final assertion of
identity in the face of those who wish to destroy him by stealing
his Name:

> I am King Congal of Connaught and of Tara,
> That wise, victorious, voluble, unlucky,
> Blasphemous, famous, infamous man.
> Fool, take this spit when red with blood,
> Show it to the people and get all the pennies;
> What does it matter what they think?
> The Great Herne knows that I have won.

This claim is of the same kind as the one made after the thunder spoke in Scene v and several times during this Scene:

> I held you in my arms last night,
> We seven held you in our arms.

It picks out of the whole truth that part of it which is the hero's truth. Congal is King Congal of Connaught and of Tara, and not a Fool. But just as the rape was a sacrament, so the hero is a fool, and has worked out his destiny according to the first stave of the curse:

> He that a herne's egg dare steal
> Shall be changed into a fool.

In the god's perspective everything from the death of Aedh to his own self-destruction has been Congal's fool's play. As Attracta says,

> You were under the curse, in all
> You did, in all you seemed to do.

But this is not the audience's perspective. They can discern what Conrad called 'the accent of heroic truth' [42] as well as the fool's play. Congal's last words are of the victorious bouts he knows and not of the logic of defeat which he is precluded from grasping:

> But I have beaten you, Great Herne,
> In spite of your kitchen spit—seven men—
> *(He dies.)*

The account I have given of the play so far has done no justice to the characterization of Attracta. She convinces us of the reality of her mystical life by her human dignity and warmth and the way in which these contrast, when she is in her trance, with the harsh and terrified abandon of her welcome to the god. Nor has another element in the play had much attention—that which is best represented by Corney, Attracta's servant, and his donkey, formerly a highwayman. The theme is developed at the end of the last Scene, after Congal's death. Because Corney's donkey has broken from where it was tethered further down the mountain and is coupling with another donkey, the hero's soul is destined to be reborn in that shape. The last words of the play are Corney's:

> All that trouble and nothing to show for it,
> Nothing but just another donkey.

This is more than a cynical footnote or afterthought, because the presence of Corney and his donkey throughout the play prepares for it. Congal's metamorphosis accords with the other indignities that cock a malicious eye at the Yeatsian Prufrock— the fight with the table-legs, the drawing of lots for Attracta, the god who is a heron and a thunder-bogy, death on a kitchen-spit. As a theme, too, metempsychosis is worked into the narrative at an earlier stage (in Corney's chatter about his donkey's past); Congal fears what the Great Herne 'May do with me when I am dead', and Attracta predicts this final punishment for his hubris (which he must share with the other campaigners who have insulted her) in Scene v. The episode may be objected to, not because it is incongruous or inconsequential, but for other reasons.

First, it turns the play in the direction of moral allegory, as any epiloguizing which insists too confidently on the protagonist's *final* place in the macrocosm will tend to do (consider the difference between *Doctor Faustus* and *Othello*). It upsets the delicate equilibrium between the god's perspective and the hero's perspective which has been the audience's angle of vision. The play begins to look like a parable about the superiority of the mystical to the heroic life: those who choose to be heroes rather than adepts will be re-born in lower forms; the mystic is released from the wheel of incarnations. With such matters Yeats was preoccupied at the time when he wrote *The Herne's Egg*. But, although in a game as in a drama one side or the other may legitimately be said to win, it seems much riskier to say that victory has proved the victor right. That is a theory which appertains to trials by combat, ideological wars, and the moral play.

Secondly, the part played by Attracta in the episode is obscure and contradictory. Congal, afraid of being put 'Into the shape of a brute beast', begs her to protect him against the Great Herne. Attracta believes that the god, whose knowledge she shares since her mystic marriage with him, has not yet determined Congal's fate, and therefore says to Corney:

> Come lie with me upon the ground,
> Come quickly into my arms, come quickly, come
> Before his body has had time to cool.

But Corney, frightened of the Herne, hesitates; his donkey breaks free, and it is too late:

CORNEY

King Congal must be born a donkey!

ATTRACTA

Because we were not quick enough.

In the light of her previous role as the god's agent, Attracta's action is inconsistent, and indeed inexplicable. For why should she attempt to frustrate his purposes? Yeats seems to have been betrayed into muddling his own design through the influence of his sources.* And the reason given for failure—'Because we were not quick enough'—suggests, with a cynicism which is jarringly ungenerous to both god and hero as they have been depicted in the play, that the Great Wheel, like other kinds of machinery, can be halted by the most trivial forms of accident.

If images are structural, what is being criticized here is structure itself. This is a measure of the seriousness with which *The Herne's Egg* needs to be taken, compared with the other plays discussed in this chapter. When *The Player Queen* was found in patches intolerably obscure this seemed to be because some parts of the plot, characterization, and symbolism had not achieved the right relation with the theme which other parts jibed with; they were bits that had fallen off or not been used, and so could not be considered part of the structure at all. They were bad because, like builder's débris, they spoiled the look of the place. In *Where There Is Nothing* there is very little that is solid at all—a mist of ideas imperfectly enclosed in a ragged envelope. But in *The Herne's Egg* all runs sweetly up to the pinnacle, which is firmly set

---

* As F. A. C. Wilson explains it (*W. B. Yeats and Tradition*, p. 108), Attracta has become since her divine union a Swedenborgian angelic spirit and in this condition tries to protect Congal. But why should an angel attempt to frustrate the god? Wilson also shows on pp. 102–4 that her presence at Congal's death also owes something to Ferguson's Lafinda in his *Congal*. Another reason for the episode may be that it allows Yeats to make a further technical discrimination between the divine marriage and human sexual union (see her speech 'I lay with the Great Herne' on p. 72). This theme, however fascinating (it is important in the Ribh poems in 'Supernatural Songs'), seems here an intrusion from the philosophical mythology.

and made of congruent material, but is wrong none the less—a wrong design for a structure which conforms to another mode of design; a moral-play epilogue to a drama of the Shakespearian kind. But its possession of this last quality, so far as it can be limited to a compassionate sense of human dignity amidst the travesties of it and the terrors, distinguishes *The Herne's Egg* from the other two plays, as it distinguishes *Purgatory*.

Chapter Eight

The Image in the Head

For wisdom is the property of the dead.

I

Y EATS wrote the prose-dialogue of *The King of the Great Clock Tower* 'that I might be forced to make lyrics for its imaginary people'.[1] Ezra Pound declared that the play was 'putrid', but Yeats was unrepentant:

> From all that makes a wise old man
> That can be praised of all;
> O what am I that I should not seem
> For the song's sake a fool.[2]

He rewrote the play in verse, and then produced a second version of the same story, *A Full Moon in March*. *The King of the Great Clock Tower* was performed at the Abbey in July, 1934: '. . . send the enclosed cutting to Ezra that I may confound him. He may have been right to condemn it as poetry but he condemned it as drama. It has turned out the most popular of my dance-plays.'[3]

A common man, 'Stroller and Fool', appears before the King and Queen:

A year ago somebody told me that you had married the most beautiful woman in the world, and from that moment I have had her image in my head, and month by month, it has grown more and more beautiful. I have made poems about her and sung them everywhere, but I have never seen her.[4]

He swears, or prophesies, that the Queen will dance for him, that he will sing for her, and that, as a reward, she will give him a kiss. The King, furious at the insult, orders him to be beheaded. The head is brought, and the King insists that the Queen shall dance:

Dance! Dance! If you are nothing to him but an image, a body in his head, he is nothing to you but a head without a body.

The Queen dances, the head sings, and the Queen 'presses her lips to the lips of the head'. The King kneels to her, lowering his sword. In *A Full Moon in March* there are only two characters, apart from the Musicians—Queen and Swineherd. The Queen orders the Swineherd to be beheaded because he has heaped 'complexities of insult' upon her. But she drops her veil and dances, holding the severed head, which sings. In all the versions, the Musicians' songs enforce the themes of the sexual joys of eternity, the 'miraculeuse nuit nuptiale' of Villiers de l'Isle-Adam's *Axël*, and of Baile and Aillinn,[5] and meditate upon the communion between the emblematic Queen and the foulness of the common man:

> What can she lack whose emblem is the moon!
> But desecration and the lover's night.

These plays have proved amenable to explanation on several different levels. For T. R. Henn, the Queen primarily represents Woman, obsessed with the sexual act, and eternally seeking ravishment; the story tells of the ultimate victory of Man over perverse and vicious Woman and her 'virgin cruelty', and of 'the poet triumphant after death through his magical and enduring art'.[6] For Frank Kermode, the Stroller / Swineherd is the *poète maudit*, and the Queen's beauty, or the Queen herself, is the Image, out of time and deathless; the dance with the severed head is a complex symbol of 'the Dancer in the special role of the Image that costs the artist personal happiness, indeed life itself'.[7] F. A. C. Wilson, while making room for Henn's interpretation, concentrates chiefly on a theological and Platonic one: the Stroller symbolizes 'spirit in its fallen condition, but spirit which is . . . nevertheless in love with the idea of Heaven', symbolized by the Queen; Eternity, too, is, in Blake's phrase, 'in love with the productions of time', and therefore the dance with the severed head 'is in one sense symbolic of the union of spirit with the principle from which it emanates'.[8]

I have mentioned these interpretations here—without, however, attempting to do them any sort of justice—because they are not incompatible with each other; something resembling the old system of tropological and anagogical readings has a highly practical value here. All interpretations of these plays are likely to share a common characteristic. The mode of existence and of action belonging to the characters is to be seen as representing something which is not overtly expressed in it. The persons behave in a manner analogous to that of participants in a rite, and the Musicians' songs can be compared to the psalms, hymns, or other prescribed chants, which accompany and, in this case, explain the general significance of what is being done. When we ask about the celebrant of a rite 'Why is he doing that?', the answer we expect is not one in terms of the priest's or the victim's personal motives or life-history but in terms of what the ritual lays down. Enquiries about the ultimate meaning of the actions are always in the end enquiries about the meanings attached to the ritual or the fable as a whole. (It is not necessary here to go into the complicated question about ritual's precedence over fable, or vice-versa.) If the priest plucks out the victim's heart, or drains the cup before the altar, explanations in terms of his cruelty or thirst are plainly out of court. The characters in these three plays are entirely submissive to the roles which the fable prescribes for them. These roles are designed not on the pattern of ordinary human action, or even in accord with such networks of recognizably human motivation and interplaying impulses as are labelled heroic legend or Noh play, but as projections of the multiple meanings of the story, Woman's Cruelty and Man's Desire, Accursed Poet and Romantic Image, Eternity and its Emanations.

In their more brashly emblematical forms the characters in this kind of drama can become like those gods and godlings which are illustrated in the Renaissance handbooks of mythology, the work of a Cartari or Natale Conti: the man with serpents instead of fingers, the woman with three animal heads, the naked man headed like a bird of prey.[9] The severed head which sings, although—or because—it has many antecedents in tradition, has an affinity with these fabulous creatures. They are mere monsters if the imagination permits them to become disjoined from the meanings which their queer properties emblematize.

It is this feature which differentiates *The King of the Great Clock Tower* and *A Full Moon in March* quite sharply from most of the plays discussed in the previous chapters. Their relation to their tale is not the same as the relation of Cuchulain or Congal, Deirdre or Seanchan, Decima or Emer, to their stories.

Indeed, a possible fault of these dance-plays is that what remains of ordinary human motivation is sometimes found in rather grotesque combination with its absence, just as mechanically realistic drawings of human anatomy or classical drapery furnish forth, in Cartari's woodcuts, creatures with vulpine heads or reptilian tails. The King in *The King of the Great Clock Tower* behaves like a jealous husband. The echo of this homely theme means nothing in the fable, but only confuses it. Yeats found the character altogether unnecessary and eliminated it in *A Full Moon in March*. I have seen no interpretation of the plays which makes it clear why the Queen should be considered, or should consider herself, insulted by the Stroller / Swineherd's somewhat tepid commendations of her beauty when at last he beholds it. What he sees when he still wears the muddy vesture of mortality and looks through corporeal eyes is not, of course, so fine as the 'image in his head' with which he will unite after death in 'the condition of fire', the conflagration of bodiless intercourse when he is 'transfigured to pure substance'.[10] He says so, and speaks boldly of that sacred dance and mysterious kiss. All this is in fitting accord with his several symbolic roles. But the Queen's reaction is less attuned to hers. In *The King of the Great Clock Tower* it is the King who is outraged by the Stroller's insolence. This is better than *A Full Moon in March*, where the Queen herself says:

> All here have heard the man and all have judged.
> I led him, that I might not seem unjust,
> From point to point, established in all eyes
> That he came hither not to sing but to heap
> Complexities of insult on my head.[11]

This is all very human and queenly, and provides the occasion for the Swineherd's punishment. But this Queen needs no excuses for her cruelty or witnesses to her justice. It is the dramatist who has needed the insult-motif as an excuse to keep his story unfolding; he 'must have severed heads',[12] and he must somehow contrive that the Queen shall behead the Swineherd in order to organize his central symbol. A touch of human motivation is introduced into the rite. This contrasts with total submission to it on the Swineherd's part. When he is told that he must die he is impassive; his death is not personal; he is neither glad nor sorry, nor fearful, nor brave; he is the Victim, and his death occasions prophecy. Long before it is off, his trunkless head has already become an emblem to himself.

These inconsistencies are forgotten by those who respond to the power of the Musicians' songs. They are amongst the most compelling of all Yeats's later poems. He has now, with perhaps a touch of pettishness, ceased to worry about whether or not the music will distort the words and prevent the audience hearing them:

I say to the musician 'Lose my words in patterns of sound as the name of God is lost in Arabian arabesques. They are a secret between the singers, myself, yourself. The plain fable, the plain prose of the dialogue, Ninette de Valois' dance are there for the audience. They can find my words in the book if they are curious, but we will not thrust our secret upon them. . . .'* [13]

There is one song in the plays which ought not to have the same character as the others, because it is a part, or fulfilment, of the action in a way that they are not. This is the song of the severed head itself. It was not until the final version that Yeats hit upon the effective way of doing this. There are two other versions of the head's song (in the two versions of *The King of the Great Clock Tower*), but they fail to be dramatic because they are like the other

---

* I interpret this passage differently from Wilson (p. 54), for whom it implies that the understanding of the songs is purposively reserved for initiates into the philosophical mythology. I think that the 'secret' which is to be kept from the audience is what the words *are*, not what they are about; the curious can discover the former if they wish and there is nothing to suggest that they may not then be read as poems; as such, they are less obscure than other late poems such as 'The Statues' and 'The Gyres'. Their function in the plays is psalmodic, accompanying the ritual, so in theory it does not matter if they are not heard in the theatre. But Yeats's apparent willingness to accept this expedient is connected with his prolonged inability to get words and music in what he considered right relation: see above, p. 116.

songs in the play, and are, indeed, interchangeable with them. But in *A Full Moon in March*, the song ('I sing a song of Jack and Jill') has the right air of inexpressive mystery—inexpressive because inexpressible like the notes sung to 'Heav'n's new-born Heir' by Milton's Cherubim. It is the depersonalized voice of phantasmic folk-song and nursery-rhyme, utterly different from the richer and more human note of amazement and longing heard in the Musicians' songs. As far as the central symbol, the dance with the severed head, is concerned, it is precisely this remoteness and inexpressibility that count. The moment has nothing at all in common with the rather frantic attempts of Oscar Wilde (which gave Yeats the hint) or of Arthur Symons to actualize the Salome incident—'Je la mordrai avec mes dents comme on mord un fruit mur', and so on.[14] All human character and circumstance sink away. Otherwise silly, shocking, or monstrous, it is clinically pure, if also rather dull, when it is related with exactitude to the mystery to come, like the Renaissance *icones symbolicae* of Chronos's self-emasculation or Saturn's eating his children. It is also, of course, extremely pagan, as the long struggle of Christianity against the Hellenizing of the incidents of the incarnation into abstract or neo-Platonic mysteries sufficiently shows. Yeats was well aware of this. In choosing an image which is, if wrongly read, morbid and offensive he was issuing a challenge, a heresiarch's demand for allegiance.

II

I have summed up the difference between these plays and most of the others as a difference in the way the characters are related to the stories. This distinction seems to be of the first importance in a general view of Yeats's drama. In *The King of the Great Clock Tower* and *A Full Moon in March* the personages are primarily projections of the fable's meanings. Their deeds and their attributes are simply clues to the meanings they are acting out. They are simulacra of human forms; they even simulate the human process by which desire leads to activity. But they have no individuality and no names, except ritual ones, any more than have Jack in the Green, the yearly Tammuz, St. George, or the Betty. Everything they do can, and should, be done again exactly as before.

There are signs in plenty of this mummer's play genre in Yeats's other dramas. *The Cat and the Moon* is perhaps the most obvious. More remotely related to the type are *The Dreaming of the Bones* and *Calvary*, especially the latter. In *The Dreaming of the Bones* the three characters combine to show forth an ancient wrong and its nexus of cause and ever-iterated consequence. But there the fixity of the roles, which is brought out by the characters' sufferings and struggles to escape, and by the soldier's momentary impulse towards departing from his own unforgiving hatred, is itself part of the play; forced to act out a meaning, the persons try to break free of the perpetual repetition of the dreadful anniversary. In *Calvary*, the play of Christ's 'dreaming-back', each character has its self-determined role; they are all paradigms of the Subjective Man's intolerance of an equally paradigmatic saviour. In other places, in the final moments of *The Herne's Egg* and in some parts of *The Player Queen*, we have noticed a similar relationship between character and the absolutely demonstrative. *The Hour-Glass*, too, a 'morality',[15] is related to this kind.

With Yeats's other plays it is no such matter. The persons confront a world which may be utterly strange to them and to us, Spenser's world of 'Infernall Hags, Centaurs, feendes, Hippodames', a Mareotic sea of Baconian εἴδωλα or neo-Platonic *icones*. It solicits weirdly, and often comprehensively denies human will or desire; but the characters are not its instruments, or, if they become so, it is not without a struggle in which individual motivation of a recognizably human kind is paramount. Deirdre, Cuchulain, Emer, Congal are individualized at least in so far as they have to choose their roles and to make, if they can, their own stories. Usually they are defeated by the world of Fand, Bricriu, Aoife and the Herne, but the protagonists themselves are not supernatural, not gods but heroes. Although 'At stroke of midnight God shall win', until that hour they endure their 'bodily or mental furniture'.[16] That is why it seems possible to discuss Yeats's drama in ways which often disregard his frequently expressed wish to 'empty' his work of the naïvely human. It is not until 'Mankind can do no more' that the personages become still, unmoving figures like Emer and Cuchulain (in *At the Hawk's Well*) and submit to 'God' or destiny or to their transformation into ghosts, animals, or images. 'I have beaten you, Great Herne' may be a deluded cry, but it is not a disillusioned one, nor, indeed, is 'Cuchulain, son of Sualtim, comes!' The supreme example of this seems to be *Purgatory*, the protagonist's struggle in 'the network of the stars', heredity and the inexorable conditions of the supernatural world. Unless we are to regard the old man's last words as merely the rhetoric appropriate to a curtain-line—which it may well be proper to do—the struggle has in this instance even transformed the God who 'wins' into a God who can be prayed to. The contrast with the Swineherd and the Severed Head is huge.

Purgatory and *A Full Moon in March*, both written in the same decade, are extreme examples of the contrary trends. They compose the antithesis on which it is entirely fitting to let any study of Yeats rest as best it may. The Severed Head knows all, and man is stricken deaf and dumb and blind:

No living man can drink from the whole wine

The old man in *Purgatory*, like the old Adam, struggles blindly, and sight, when it is finally purged, puts an end to his day's war, but

A living man is blind and drinks his drop.

Notes

THESE Notes are normally confined to references to quotations or allusions in the text, where some longer Notes (indicated by *) will be found. The following abbreviations are used for the more frequently cited works, all of which are by Yeats except the last five:

C.K.   *The Countess Kathleen and Various Legends and Lyrics* (London, 1892).
C.P.   *Collected Poems* (London, 1934 edn.).
C. Plays *Collected Plays* (London, 1934)
C.W.   *Collected Works* (Stratford-on-Avon, 1908), eight volumes.
D.P.   *Dramatis Personae 1896–1902—Estrangement—The Death of Synge—The Bounty of Sweden* (London, 1936).
F.P.D. *Four Plays for Dancers* (London, 1921).
Letters   *The Letters of W. B. Yeats*, ed. Allan Wade (London, 1954).
L.P.P.   *Last Poems and Plays* (London, 1940).
P. & C. *Plays and Controversies* (London, 1923).
P.P.V. *Plays in Prose and Verse Written for an Irish Theatre and Generally with the Help of a Friend* (London, 1922).
W. & B. *Wheels and Butterflies* (London, 1934).
Ellis-Fermor Una Ellis-Fermor, *The Irish Dramatic Movement* (London, 1954 edn.).
Henn   T. R. Henn, *The Lonely Tower—Studies in the Poetry of W. B. Yeats* (London, 1950).
Parkinson Thomas Parkinson, *W. B. Yeats Self-Critic—A Study of his Early Verse* (Berkeley & Los Angeles, 1951).
Wade   Allan Wade, *A Bibliography of the Writings of W. B. Yeats* (London, 1951; 2nd edn., 1957).
Wilson   F. A. C. Wilson, *W. B. Yeats and Tradition* (London, 1958).

CHAPTER ONE

[1] *Samhain*, October 1901, p. 12.
[2] *D.P.*, p. 33.
[3] Lady Gregory, *Our Irish Theatre* (New York, 1914), pp. 20–1.
[4] *Literary Ideals in Ireland* (London and Dublin), 1899, p. 87.
[5] Quoted by Wade, p. 260.
[6] W. G. Fay and C. Carswell, *The Fays of the Abbey Theatre* (London, 1935), pp. 112–13.
[7] *D.P.*, p. 35.
[8] *P. & C.*, pp. 186–7.
[9] *D.P.*, pp. 34–5.
[10] *C.K.*, pp. 7–8.
[11] *P. & C.*, p. vi.
[12] *L.P.P.*, p. 80.
[13] Henn, p. 24.
[14] J. M. Hone, *W. B. Yeats 1865–1939* (London, 1942), pp. 87–8.
[15] *Letters*, p. 125.
[16] Maud Gonne, *A Servant of the Queen* (Dublin, 1950 edn.), p. 169. This was in 1891, according to Maud Gonne.
[17] *Letters*, p. 108. The 'folklore book' is *Fairy and Folk Tales of the Irish Peasantry* (1888)
[18] *P. & C.*, p. 287; compare *Fairy and Folk Tales*, p. 233.
[19] H. S. Krans, *W. B. Yeats and the Irish Literary Revival* (New York, 1904), p. 142, Cf. E. A. Boyd, *Ireland's Literary Renaissance* (London, 1923 edn.), pp. 146–7: 'the supreme moment of Kathleen's sacrifice passes almost unnoticed'.
[20] They were suggested to Yeats by a French drawing: see *Pages from a Diary Written in 1930* (Dublin, 1944), p. 19.
[21] *Poems* (1912 edn.), p. vi.
[22] A. Symons, *Plays, Acting, and Music* (London, 1909 edn.), p. 167.
[23] This alternative version was first printed in *Poems* (1912 edn.), pp. 315–19.
[24] Robinson, 'The Man and the Dramatist' in *Scattering Branches*, ed. S. Gwynn (London, 1940), p. 87.
[25] 'The Lover Tells of the Rose in his Heart', *C.P.*, p. 62.
[26] *P. & C.*, p. 218.
[27] *C.K.*, p. 79.

CHAPTER TWO

[1] *Letters*, p. 674.
[2] *Poems* (1912 edn.), p. vi.
[3] *Letters*, p. 409.
[4] See D. M. Hoare, *The Works of Morris and of Yeats in Relation to Early Saga Literature* (Cambridge, 1937), p. 120.
[5] Preface to Vol. III of *Plays for an Irish Theatre*. This acknowledgement was not repeated in any later edition.

6 See J. H. Pollock, *William Butler Yeats* (London and Dublin, 1935), p. 46.
7 *Literary Ideals in Ireland* (London and Dublin, 1899), p. 19.
8 *Poems 1899–1905* (1906), p. 279.
9 Ellis-Fermor, p. 94.
10 'Among School Children', *C.P.*, p. 243.
11 *P.P.V.*, p. 243.
12 *P.P.V.*, p. 110; *C. Plays*, p. 141.
13 *Poems 1899–1905* (1906), pp. xi–xii.
14 This and the following quotations up to the end of the chapter are from the earliest version as printed in the 'Abbey Theatre Series', Volume V (Dublin, 1905).
15 Shakespeare, *Richard II*, II. i. 8.

CHAPTER THREE

1 Hoare, *The Works of Morris and of Yeats in Relation to Early Saga Literature* (Cambridge, 1937), pp. 130, 131.
2 Henn, p. 83.
3 L. MacNeice, *The Poetery of W. B. Yeats* (London, 1941), p. 191.
4 Ellis-Fermor, p. 115.
5 See R. Peacock, *The Poet in the Theatre* (London, 1946), p. 107.
6 Robinson, 'The Man and the Dramatist' in *Scattering Branches*, ed. S. Gwynn (London, 1940), p. 96.
7 *Letters*, p. 475.
8 *Essays* (1924), p. 328.
9 *P. & C.*, p. 124.
10 Parkinson, pp. 85–90
11 *P. & C.*, p. 151.
12 *P. & C.*, pp. 99–100.
13 *P. & C.*, p. 103.
14 *P. & C.*, p. 105.
15 *P. & C.*, p. 93.
16 *P. & C.*, p. 91.
17 *D.P.*, p. 89.
18 *P. & C.*, p. 158.
19 *D.P.*, p. 137.
20 *P. & C.*, p. 120.
21 *P. & C.*, p. 126.
22 *P. & C.*, p. 20.
23 *P. & C.*, p. 134.
24 *P. & C.*, p. 117.
25 *P. & C.*, p. 161.
26 *P. & C.*, p. 158.
27 *Essays* (1924), p. 338.
28 *The Green Helmet* (*C. Plays*, p. 243).
29 Ellis-Fermor, p. 86.

[30] *Essays* (1924), p. 297.
[31] Preface to *Plays for an Irish Theatre* (Stratford-on-Avon, 1911), pp. ix–x. This Preface, first printed in 1910 (see Wade, p. 99), is another version of the essay in *The Cutting of an Agate* (first published, New York, 1912) on 'The Tragic Theatre'.
[32] *Essays* (1924), p. 295.
[33] Preface to *Plays for an Irish Theatre* (1911), p. ix.
[34] *New Irish Comedies*, pp. 158–9, quoted Ellis-Fermor, p. 66.
[35] *D.P.*, p. 89.
[36] *D.P.*, p. 89.

CHAPTER FOUR

[1] *P. & C.*, p. 148.
[2] *L.P.P.*, p. 111.
[3] *Cuchulain of Muirthemne* (London, 1903 edn.), pp. 313–19.
[4] Parkinson, p. 80.
[5] See *Letters*, pp. 444, 595, 914.
[6] See, for example, V. K. Narayana Menon, *The Development of W. B. Yeats* (Edinburgh and London, 1942), p. 83.
[7] *In the Seven Woods* (Dublin, Cuala Press, 1903), p. 36.
[8] Parkinson, p. 54.
[9] *Poems 1899–1905*, p. 112.
[10] *Ibid.*, pp. 96–7.
[11] *Ibid.*, p. 102.
[12] *P. & C.*, p. 46.
[13] B. Bjersby, *The Interpretation of the Cuchulain Legend in the Works of W. B. Yeats* (Upsala, 1950), p. 33.
[14] *The Golden Helmet* in *C. W.*, IV. 67, 78.
[15] *Letters*, p. 674.
[16] *C. W.*, IV. 78.
[17] *F.P.D.*, pp. 17–18. All my quotations from *At the Hawk's Well* are from this edition.
[18] Henn, p. 263.
[19] *F.P.D.*, p. 42; *L.P.P.*, p. 119.
[20] Bjersby, *op. cit.*, p. 40; Pearce in *E.L.H.*, XVIII (1951).
[21] *L.P.P.*, p. 112.
[22] Praz, *The Romantic Agony* (London, 1933), p. 31.
[23] *F.P.D.*, p. 22.
[24] *F.P.D.*, p. 46.
[25] *W. & B.*, p. 75.
[26] *C. Plays*, p. 289.
[27] *F.P.D.*, p. 105.
[28] W. Y. Tindall, *The Literary Symbol* (Bloomington, 1955), pp. 181–2.
[29] Bjersby, op. cit., pp. 154–60.
[30] *W. & B.*, p. 69.
[31] Lady Gregory, *Cuchulain of Muirthemne*, ed., cit., p. 344.

[32] *Letters*, pp. 917–18.
[33] See *F.P.D.*, p. 86.
[34] Wilson, p. 163.
[35] *L.P.P.*, pp. 113–14. All my quotations from *The Death of Cuchulain* are from this edition.
[36] Wilson, p. 170.
[37] *Cuchulain of Muirthemne*, ed. cit., p. 332.

CHAPTER FIVE

[1] *Letters*, p. 627.
[2] Above, pp. 76–77.
[3] *Visions and Beliefs* (New York and London), II, 318.
[4] *Essays* (1924), pp. 526–7.
[5] *A Vision* (1925), p. 222.
[6] *F.P.D.*, p. 129.
[7] *Visions and Beliefs*, II. 300.
[8] *Ibid.*, II. 318.
[9] *Ibid.*, II. 302.
[10] *Essays* (1924), p. 520.
[11] *A Vision* (1925), p. 221; compare the Severed Head's song, *A Full Moon in March* (London, 1935), pp. 38–9.
[12] *Essays* (1924), p. 520.
[13] *Ibid.*, p. 523.
[14] *A Vision* (1925), p. 227.
[15] *Essays* (1924), p. 287.
[16] The whole idea of the play, though with important variations, is sketched out in the story 'Hanrahan's Vision': see *C.W.*, V. 248–9.
[17] *F.P.D.*, p. 65. All my quotations from the play are from this text.
[18] *Letters*, p. 626, 653, 788.
[19] 'Fenollosa on the Noh' in *The Translations of Ezra Pound* (London, 1953), pp. 279–80.
[20] *Essays* (1924), p. 289; see also Miner, *op. cit.*, pp. 256–7.
[21] *Ibid.*, p. 287.
[22] *The Translations of Ezra Pound*, pp. 283–4.
[23] *Essays* (1924), p. 285.
[24] *F.P.D.*, p. 62.
[25] *F.P.D.*, p. 63.
[26] *Letters*, p. 626, 653.
[27] *A Vision* (1925), p. 225.
[28] *Ibid.* (1925), p. 227.
[29] Frank Kermode, *Romantic Image* (London, 1957), p. 78.
[30] See Virginia Moore, *The Unicorn* (New York, 1954), pp. 225–39.
[31] *W. & B.*, p. 31.
[32] *W. & B.*, pp. 47–8. All my quotations from *The Words upon the Window-pane* are from this text.

³³ A. N. Jeffares, *W. B. Yeats: Man and Poet* (London, 1949), pp. 263–4.
³⁴ R. Ellmann, *Yeats: the Man and the Masks* (London, 1949), p. 270.
³⁵ *W. & B.*, p. 7.
³⁶ *L.P.P.*, p. 106.
³⁷ In the passage quoted above, p. 98.
³⁸ I must here withdraw what I wrote about this topic in my *Towards a Mythology* (Liverpool and London, 1946), pp. 83–4.
³⁹ *W. & B.*, p. 32. For Yeats on 'dramatization' see also L. A. G. Strong, *Green Memory* (1961), pp. 249–51.
⁴⁰ *C. W.*, V. 59–61.
⁴¹ *Autobiographies* (1926), p. 66; *W. & B.*, p. 37.
⁴² See Hone, *W. B. Yeats, 1865–1939* (London, 1942), pp. 283–4.
⁴³ *L.P.P.*, p. 97. All my quotations from *Purgatory* are from this text.
⁴⁴ *L.P.P.*, p. 102.
⁴⁵ *Wilson*, p. 152.

CHAPTER SIX

¹ See especially Henn, pp. 194–5, 268–9; Ellmann, *The Identity of Yeats* (London, 1954), pp. 260–3; Wilson, pp. 58–68.
² 'A Dialogue of Self and Soul', *C.P.*, p. 266.
³ *A Vision*, 1925, pp. 113–14.
⁴ 'A Dialogue of Self and Soul', *C.P.*, p. 265.
⁵ *A Vision*, 1925, p. 186. I have discussed the working of this idea in 'Demon and Beast' in *Irish Writing*, no. 31 (1955), pp. 42–50.
⁶ See my 'Yeats and the Prophecy of Eunapius', *Notes and Queries*, New Series, I (1954), 358–9.
⁷ Preface to *The Poetical Works* (New York, 1907), II. v.
⁸ *W. B. Yeats and T. Sturge Moore*, ed. U. Bridge (London, 1953), p. 40.
⁹ *F.P.D.*, p. 72. All my quotations from *Calvary* are from this text.
¹⁰ *Essays* (1924), p. 278.
¹¹ Preface to *The Poetical Works* (New York, 1907), II. v.
¹² *F.P.D.*, p. 76.
¹³ *A Vision* (1925), p. 187.
¹⁴ *W. & B.*, p. 118; see below, p. 122.
¹⁵ Hone, *W. B. Yeats, 1865–1939* (London, 1942), p. 417.
¹⁶ *Letters*, p. 780.
¹⁷ *P. & C.*, p. 99.
¹⁸ *W. & B.*, p. 116. All my quotations from *The Resurrection* are from this text.
¹⁹ Miner, *op. cit.*, p. 260.
²⁰ L. MacNeice, *Poetry of W. B. Yeats* (London, 1941), p. 196.
²¹ *W. & B.*, p. 109.
²² *W. & B.*, p. 110.
²³ *A Vision* (1937 edn.), p. 53.
²⁴ *Essays* (1924), p. 274.

CHAPTER SEVEN

¹ *W. & B.*, p. 101.
² *C.W.*, VII. 46.
³ *Essays* (1924), p. 301.
⁴ *C.W.*, V. 258.
⁵ *C.W.*, VII. 145.
⁶ *C.W.*, VII. 155.
⁷ *C.W.*, VII. 260, V. 223.
⁸ *C.W.*, VII. 117.
⁹ *A Vision* (1937 edn.), p. 50.
¹⁰ The best treatment of this side of Yeats's art is G. Melchiori, *The Whole Mystery of Art* (1960), pp. 35–98.
¹¹ *Where There Is Nothing: Being Volume One of Plays for an Irish Theatre* (London, 1903), pp. 46, 45. All my quotations are from this, the only, version.
¹² *Ibid.*, p. 65.
¹³ *Ibid.*, p. 98.
¹⁴ Ellis-Fermor, pp. 104–7.
¹⁵ Yeats told the story of its origin and composition on several occasions: see *C.W.*, III. 220–1; *P.P.V.*, pp. 425–7; *D.P.*, pp. 70–3.
¹⁶ *Letters*, p. 503.
¹⁷ *C.W.*, III. 198–9.
¹⁸ 'The Choice', *C.P.*, p. 278.
¹⁹ *Autobiographies* (1926), p. 388.
²⁰ *P.P.V.*, pp. 428–9.
²¹ *Essays* (1924), p. 493.
²² *Essays* (1924), p. 496.
²³ The pioneer analysis of the play is that by W. Becker, 'The Mask Mocked: or, Farce and the Dialectic of the Self' (*Sewanee Review*, LXI [1953], 82–108). Becker seems to me to make the play sound better and clearer than it is. It will be obvious that I do not agree with his view that most of the plays by Yeats preceding it 'must be relegated to the dead past'.
²⁴ *C. Plays*, p. 404. All my quotations from *The Player Queen* are from this revised final edn.
²⁵ See p. 124 above, and *A Vision* (1937 edn.), p. 268.
²⁶ *C.P.*, p. 141.
²⁷ *Early Poems and Stories* (London, 1925), p. 522.
²⁸ *Autobiographies* (1926), p. 2.
²⁹ *Essays 1931–6* (Dublin, Cuala Press, 1937), p. 129.
³⁰ Wilson, p. 182.
³¹ *Where There Is Nothing*, ed. cit., Act I.
³² *The Whole Mystery of Art*, p. 67.
³³ *C. Plays*, p. 421.
³⁴ *Essays* (1924), p. 500.
³⁵ From an unpublished notebook, quoted by Jeffares, *W. B. Yeats Man and Poet*, p. 335.
³⁶ Wilson, p. 182.

[37] Wilson, p. 183.

[38] *Pagan Mysteries in the Renaissance* (London, 1958), p. 22.

[39] N. Newton, 'Yeats as Dramatist: *The Player Queen*', *Essays in Criticism* VIII (1958).

[40] *Letters*, pp. 843, 845.

[41] *The Herne's Egg* (London, 1938), p. 10. All my quotations from the play are from this text.

[42] For Conrad's comments on this phrase of Marcus Aurelius, see 'A Familiar Preface' to *A Personal Record* (London, 1946 edn.), p. xii.

CHAPTER EIGHT

[1] *The King of the Great Clock Tower, Commentaries and Poems* (Dublin, Cuala Press, 1934), p. [iii].

[2] *Ibid.*, p. [v].

[3] *Letters*, p. 827.

[4] *The King of the Great Clock Tower*, ed. cit., p. 3.

[5] de l'Isle-Adam *Œuvres complètes* (Paris, 1923), IV. 263; see my 'Yeats's Supernatural Songs', *R.E.S.*, N.S., VII (1956).

[6] Henn, p. 270.

[7] *Romantic Image* (London, 1957), pp. 80–1, 73.

[8] Wilson, pp. 71, 78.

[9] See V. Cartari, *Le Imagini . . .* (Padua, n.d. [?1603]), pp. 105, 107, 400.

[10] 'Ribh at the Tomb . . .', *A Full Moon in March* (London, 1935), p. 61.

[11] *Ibid.*, p. 12.

[12] See *L.P.P.*, p. 112.

[13] *The King of the Great Clock Tower*, ed. cit., p. 19.

[14] Wilde, *Salomé* (London, 1927 edn.), p. 88; compare Symons, 'The Dance of the Daughters of Herodias', 'Salome' (*Collected Works* [London, 1924], II. 36, III. 239).

[15] The play is thus subtitled in earlier editions (e.g. *C.W.*, IV. 3).

[16] See 'Ribh Considers Christian Love Insufficient' and 'The Four Ages of Man', *A Full Moon in March*, ed. cit., pp. 66, 69.

Appendix: A Brief Chronology

For further information see G. B. Saul, *Prolegomena to the Study of Yeats's Plays*, Philadelphia, 1958.

* indicates plays in which Lady Gregory is known to have collaborated.

C.P. = published by the Cuala Press, Dublin.

Title of Play	Written	First Performed	First Printed
At the Hawk's Well	1915–	Lady Cunard's drawing-room, 1916	*Harper's Bazaar*, March, 1917.
Calvary	?1920		*Four Plays for Dancers* (London), 1921.
The Cat and the Moon	?1917	Abbey, 1926 (?); or 1931	*Criterion, Dial*, July, 1924.
* *Cathleen Ni Houlihan*	1901	St. Teresa's Hall, Dublin, 1902	*Samhain*, 1902.
The Countess Cathleen	1889–	Antient Concert Rooms, Dublin, 1899	*Countess Kathleen and Various Legends and Lyrics*, 1892.
The Death of Cuchulain	1938	Abbey, 1949	*Last Poems and Two Plays* (C.P.), 1939.
Deirdre	1905–	Abbey, 1906	*Deirdre* (London and Dublin), 1907.
The Dreaming of the Bones	1917	Abbey, 1931	*Two Plays for Dancers* (C.P.), *Little Review*, January, 1919.

Appendix: A Brief Chronology

Title of Play	Written	First Performed	First Printed
Fighting the Waves	1927	Abbey, 1929	*Wheels and Butterflies* (London), 1934.
A Full Moon in March	1934		*Poetry* (Chicago), 1935.
The Golden Helmet	1907	Abbey, 1908	*The Golden Helmet* (New York), 1908; *Collected Works* (Stratford), 1908.
The Green Helmet	1909	Abbey, 1910	*The Green Helmet and Other Poems* (C.P.), 1910.
The Herne's Egg	1935–		*The Herne's Egg* (London), 1938.
The Hour-glass [prose version]	1902–	Molesworth Hall, Dublin, 1903	*North American Review*, September, 1903.
The Hour-glass [poetic version]	1903–	Abbey, 1912	*The Mask* (Florence), April, 1913.
The King of the Great Clock Tower [prose version]	1933	Abbey, 1934	*The King of the Great Clock Tower Commentaries and Poems* (C.P.), 1934, *Life and Letters*, November, 1934.
The King of the Great Clock Tower [poetic version]	1934		*A Full Moon in March* (London), 1935.
*King Oedipus	1905–	Abbey, 1926	*Sophocles' King Oedipus* (London), 1928.
*The King's Threshold	1903	Molesworth Hall, Dublin, 1903	*The King's Threshold* (New York), 1904, *The King's Threshold and On Baile's Strand* (London and Dublin), 1904.

Appendix: A Brief Chronology

Title of Play	Written	First Performed	First Printed
The Land of Heart's Desire	1894	Avenue Theatre, London, 1894	The Land of Heart's Desire (London), also Chicago, 1894.
Oedipus at Colonus	1926–	Abbey, 1927	Collected Plays (London), 1934.
*On Baile's Strand	1901–	Abbey, 1904	In the Seven Woods (Dun Emer Press, Dundrum), 1903.
The Only Jealousy of Emer	1916	publicly staged in Amsterdam in 1922 by Albert van Dalsum	Poetry (Chicago), January, 1919.
The Player Queen	1908–	King's Hall, London (Stage Society), 1919	The Dial, November, 1922
*The Pot of Broth	1902	Antient Concert Rooms, Dublin, 1902	Plays in Prose and Verse (London), 1922.
Purgatory	1938	Abbey, 1938	Last Poems and Two Plays (C.P.), 1939.
The Resurrection	1925–	Abbey, 1934	Adelphi (London), June, 1927.
The Shadowy Waters	ca. 1885–	Molesworth Hall, Dublin, 1904	North American Review, May, 1900.
The Shadowy Waters [acting version]	1906	Abbey, 1906	The Shadowy Waters (London), 1907.
*The Unicorn from the Stars	1907	Abbey, 1907	The Unicorn from the Stars and Other Plays (New York), 1908.

Appendix: A Brief Chronology

Title of Play	Written	First Performed	First Pinted
* l, here There Is Nothing	1902	Royal Court Theatre, London (Stage Society), 1904	United Irishman, 1902.
The Words upon the Window-pane	1930	Abbey, 1930	The Words upon the Window Pane (C.P.), 1934.

Index